W9-BCQ-323

elements

jason roberts food

gardenelements

morningelements

earthelements

oceanelements

elements

jason roberts food

photography by oliver ford

When I was growing up, I always wanted to cook. And because there were members of my family who worked in catering and ran a restaurant, I probably had the "foodie gene" built-in. So for as long as I can remember, I loved experimenting with food. I'd try out all kinds of combinations then I'd get my family or school friends to sample my latest creation.

It occurred to me fairly early that it's not just about preparing the food—although I find that extremely rewarding—it's equally about the element of sharing it with others. I even shared with my dog when things didn't quite turn out.

But what this constant experimentation taught me was a passion for combining food elements to their greatest effect. I love creating taste sensations, delicate textures and mouth-watering flavours. I love that there's such an enormous variety of fresh produce, spices and herbs to make delicious, nutritious and wholesome meals. And I love to have fun doing it and enjoying it with others.

I sometimes think the pace of life makes us forget the joy of being in the kitchen. The happy atmosphere, food simmering on the

life's elements

stove, the aromas, a drink with old friends, a laugh, a wonderful meal, and a very good time.

That's essentially what this book is about—bringing all the elements together in a celebration every day.

Most of my recipes are quick and easy to prepare using readily available ingredients—often simple elements you're likely to have in your pantry. There are also some recipes you might find a little more challenging. Trust me though, they too are well worth the effort.

I hope my book inspires you to spend more time in your kitchen with your family and friends. For me, food is one of life's most enjoyable elements. Come and join me explore it.

Jason

CONTENTS elements

breakfastelements

I know it's a bit old now saying that "breakfast is the most important meal of the day", but it really is! I live by that saying.

I find that without a good feed to start the day, I tend to reach a point where I feel lethargic and tired and my brain doesn't think as quickly as I'd like it too.

A good-sized bowl of my Freight Train Muesli is highly recommended. A little roughage with a touch of added fibre is not only good for your insides, but gets your metabolism going and the party started.

I also love breakfast because it lends itself to family time—eating breakfast allows for communication.

I love that saying: "families that eat together, stay together".

Freight Train Muesli

I call this Freight Train Muesli because it literally goes through you like a freight train. It is so important to start the day with a good wholesome fibrous breakfast. Not only is it important to break-the-fast but just to start the day with something nourishing to give you energy and get your metabolism levels up… and it tastes great.

2½ cups (225g/8 oz) rolled oats

½ cup (80g/2¾ oz) sunflower seeds

½ cup (80g/2¾ oz) pumpkin seeds

½ cup (70g/2½ oz) slivered almonds

½ cup (70g/2½ oz) hazelnuts

½ cup (125ml/4 fl oz) maple syrup*

¼ cup (45g/1½ oz) dried figs (try and get the Persian ones, they're so delicious)

¼ cup (35g/1¼ oz) dried apricots

¼ cup (45g /1½ oz) raisins or sultanas

¼ cup (45g/1½ oz) chopped crystallised ginger, optional

1 tsp Flax seeds or psyllium husk (both optional).

Pre heat oven to 170°C/340°F.

Place oats, seeds and nuts in a large baking dish. Sprinkle over the maple syrup and fold through evenly with a fork. Cook until a light golden colour is reached, approximately 15 to 20 minutes, stirring occasionally.

Allow time to cool before adding remaining ingredients. To serve, top with fresh fruit, yoghurt and milk if desired.

Add a teaspoon of flax seeds or psyllium husk when serving, for extra fibre.

Serves: This quantity will serve 2 over a 5 to 6 day period

Notes: *Alternatively you could dilute honey with a bit of orange or pineapple juice.

Storage suggestion: Store in an airtight container and the muesli will keep relatively fresh for up to 2 weeks in a cupboard.

Bircher Muesli with Toasted Coconut and Mango

Serves: 4

***Note:** If mangoes are unavailable, bananas or berries work fine too!

I love my cereal and I love my sport!

What I love about Bircher muesli is the concept of making it the night before. Getting up in the morning, going surfing, running or swimming, whatever I'm into at the moment, then coming home to a good helping of Bircher muesli topped with toasted coconut and fresh mango.

2 cups ((80g/6⅓ oz) (organic) rolled oats
⅓ cup (50g/1¾ oz) toasted sesame seeds
1 cup (250ml/8 fl oz) (organic) apple juice
1 cup (150g/5⅓ oz) coarsely grated apple
½ cup (140g/5⅓ oz)s natural yoghurt
Juice of 1 grapefruit
⅓ cup (15g/½ oz) toasted, flaked coconut
1 large mango*

Place oats, sesame seeds and apple juice in a bowl and soak for an hour, or overnight, if time permits.

Add grated apple, yoghurt and grapefruit juice to the mixture and mix well.

Spoon into serving bowls and top with coconut and half a mango, cut into thick slices.

"best day of my life" is my favourite quote after i have that sort of a start to the day!

Smoked Salmon Pancakes

This is one of those impressive dishes that your friends will want the recipe for. Certainly not a high fibre breakfast but a decadent one to remember. This dish works perfectly as a hors d'oeuvre by simply making bite sized portions.

Serves: 4

1 egg
½ cup (125ml/4 fl oz) milk
2 tbs (40ml/1⅓rd fl oz) olive oil
80g (2¾ oz) plain flour
1 tsp baking powder (baking soda)
pinch of salt and freshly ground black pepper, to taste
Butter, for cooking
200g (7 oz) smoked salmon
1 small Spanish onion (red), finely sliced
¼ cup, washed and drained baby capers
½ cup (120g/4¼ oz) light sour cream
Cracked pepper
1 cup rocket leaves (arugula) leaves

Using a fork whisk the eggs, milk and olive oil until well combined.

In another bowl, sift the dry ingredients together. Gradually pour in the egg mixture and lightly beat until smooth. Set aside to rest for 30 minutes.

Heat a non-stick pan with a little butter over a medium heat. When foam subsides, drop in approximately 4 heaped spoons of pancake batter, lifting and tilting pan to evenly spread the mixture. Cook until bubbles appear on the surface of the pancake. Flip and cook until golden on the other side. Keep warm in low oven while cooking remaining pancakes.

To serve, lay the smoked salmon over the pancake to create a complete thin layer. Scatter each serving with a little of the onion, capers and a small quenelle (or scoop) of the sour cream. To finish, crack over fresh black pepper and a scattering of rocket leaves.

Poached Pears with Star Anise and Ruby Grapefruit

Serves: 4

Note: The vanilla and star anise are optional flavourings.

When it comes to finding the right pear, it should be soft but not mushy, firm but not hard.

When it comes to winter and its fruit, I am a little partial to the humble pear. Simple, elegant and beautifully textured, especially when poached to perfection.

Combined with the tang of some plump, juicy grapefruit segments and toasted almonds, the word is HEAVEN.

Vanilla and Almond cream

1 vanilla bean

1 x 200g (7 oz) tub light vanilla yoghurt

¼ cup (35g/1¼ oz) toasted, slivered almonds

4 firm but ripe pears

1 litre (32 fl oz) cold water

250g (8¾ oz) raw sugar

2 star anise (spice)

1 ruby grapefruit

1 papaya (or paw paw)

Split vanilla bean in half. Scrape out the seeds (reserving the pod) and place in a bowl with the yoghurt and almonds. Mix well and refrigerate.

To poach the pears; peel, halve and remove the core. Place in a small saucepan, covered with water, sugar, star anise, reserved vanilla pod and a couple of pieces of zest from the Ruby grapefruit. Cover with a piece of greaseproof paper.

Place the pan over a medium to high flame and bring to the boil. Once it has reached boiling point remove from heat and allow to cool for at least an hour, this will enable the pears to carry on cooking.

Prepare the grapefruit by removing the skin and pith all in one go, using a small knife. Using your knife, cut each side of the dividing membrane to remove each segment. It may sound hard, but it's not. You are trying to refine the grapefruit's texture.

Split the papaya in half, remove skin and the seeds. Cut into wedges. To serve, mix a little of the pear syrup with the pears and grapefruit segments and place a serving in each bowl. Dollop with some of the vanilla and almond cream.

Cheats Omelette #2

The cheats omelette was a huge success in my first book *Graze*, so I thought I would put a variation of it in *Elements*.

For those of you who aren't familiar, as peculiar as it sounds, this works! Adjust the ingredients depending on how many you're cooking for.

Serves: This recipe is per person

Note: This is also a favourite for camping, fishing and college dorms!

2 eggs, per person

½ a small potato, cooked and cut into cubes

1 sprig rosemary, leaves removed and finely chopped (or $^{1}/_{2}$ tsp dried)

1 tbs grated Parmesan cheese

30g (1 oz) Fontina cheese, cut into little cubes (substitute Mozzarella or Taleggio if you prefer)

Salt and freshly ground black pepper, to taste

16x10cm (6⅓ x 4 inch) Ziploc® bag

20

Place all ingredients in the Ziploc® bag. Season, close the bag and mix ingredients together with your hands and then shake well.

Drop bag into a pot of boiling water and cook until set. The cooking time will vary depending on your method of heat, however should be around 15 minutes. The omelette is cooked when firm.

Remove by cutting the top of the bag with a sharp knife. Serve immediately, preferably with lashings of rocket (arugula) doused in extra virgin olive oil and a little lemon juice or as a nice addition to a salad.

Corn Cakes With Pancetta And Avocado

Serves: 2 (2 per person)

Notes: Pancetta is an Italian style bacon cured with salt, pepper and other spices. It is not smoked. Bacon is taken from the back, sides and belly of the pig and may be smoked. Pancetta is a made from the belly only and is often sold in a sausage-like roll.

Many cafés in Sydney Australia will serve hot corn cakes, and so they should, they are absolutely delicious! I love using sweet corn kernels, freshly cut from the cob, along with a little spice (hence the cayenne)! If fresh corn isn't available, by all means use canned corn. Just add a pinch of sugar to the batter.

1 cob sweet corn or 200gms tinned drained corn (corn kernels)

4 thin slices of rolled pancetta* or 4 rashers of streaky bacon

1 tbs extra virgin olive oil

80 ml milk

80 g plain flour, sifted

1 egg

1 tsp baking powder

Pinch of cayenne pepper

3-4 large basil leaves, washed & finely shredded

Sea salt & freshly ground black pepper

1 tbs olive oil, extra, (for cooking)

1 firm but ripe avocado, sliced

Extra basil leaves for garnish

2 tbs sour cream, preferably reduced fat (optional)

Peel (shuck) the husk away from the cob of corn and remove the silk threads from along the kernels. Using a sharp knife, remove the corn kernels from the cob. Reserve.

Cook pancetta, or bacon, under a moderately hot grill until crisp. Alternatively place on a wire rack over a baking tray and cook in a moderately hot oven (180°C) until crisp, or simply panfry till golden. Drain well on absorbent paper. Reserve.

In a medium size mixing bowl. Combine olive oil, milk, flour, egg, baking powder and cayenne pepper. Using a fork, mix batter well to combine, break down any lumps.

Add the corn and basil to the batter, fold through until evenly distributed. Season to taste.

Heat remaining olive oil in a large non-stick pan until moderately hot.

Divide batter into four and spoon (fritter style) into pan. Cook corn cakes, flipping, until golden on both surfaces. Keep warm until ready to serve.

Serve corn cakes topped with crisp pancetta and sliced avocado. Garnish with fresh basil leaves.

If you're feeling a little decadent, add a dollop of sour cream.

Glass of Breakfast

Here's a delicious way to start the day. Packed with fibre, energy and anti-oxidants this little kick-start is so easy to make. You may find blueberries quite pricey when out of season. I often have a box of frozen blueberries at hand for when they're too expensive or out of season. Strawberries and raspberries are certainly just as delicious.

Serves: 2 large portions

Note: For the lactose intolerant, soy based products work just super.

1 cup (250ml/8 fl oz) light/low fat milk

½ cup (140g/5 oz) (acidophilus) yoghurt

1 ripe banana, peeled and chopped

1 cup blueberries

2 tbs almond meal

2 tsp wheat germ

24

In a blender, combine all the ingredients and process until smooth.
Serve immediately.

Fresh Fruit Plate

This dish is a 'no brainer' for most. For some it can be an absolute triumph with a symphony of seasonal flavours and others an absolute flop.

In my opinion the fruit plate should represent the ripest of fruit in each particular season. This book is being shot during the summer months in Australia when we have an eclectic mix of fruit to choose from, everything from nectarines to cherries, lychees to mangosteens.

It would be silly for me to write a recipe and expect you to try and find the fruit I have chosen if you live in Grand Rapids, Michigan and it's snowing. The best way to come up with a fruit plate is to go to your local market and find inspiration in what smells and looks ripe.

I certainly prefer my fruit at room temperature for breakfast, so depending on ripeness, try and leave the fruit out the night before, thus taking away the chill.

OK, now I'm going to have a whinge… and it doesn't happen often. I have a pet hate of fruit salad that is full of apples and oranges and has been chopped to death. I love big shards of impeccably cut fruit that I can pick up with my hands, that's just me though. Make your own decision, but just keep in mind that the fruit tastes so much better when it's ripe.

Baked Peaches With Fresh Ricotta

This dish may look simple given the few ingredients and it doesn't require a great deal of skill. It is important that the peaches are impeccably ripe for them to bake to a jam like consistency, the ricotta is fresher than tomorrow and the 2nd track of Bernard Fannings new CD is up loud and the sun is shining.

If ever you're in Haberfield, Sydney Australia, go and check out PAESANELLA cheese manufacturers. I kid you not, the best ricotta to have blessed this earth.

Serves: 2

* **Note:** Verjuice is unfermented grape juice.

3 large ripe peaches (preferably free stone)
½ cup (125ml/4 fl oz) verjuice* or unsweetened apple juice
1 tbs brown sugar
2 cinnamon sticks
1 fresh lime
½ cup (125g/4 oz) fresh ricotta

28

Pre heat oven to 170°C/340°F. Using a sharp knife split the peaches in half, removing the stone.

Lay into a baking dish cut side up, drizzle over verjuice, scatter with brown sugar and cinnamon sticks and place into oven for about 20 to 25 minutes. The peaches should soften but not burst.

Allow to cool for a good 10 minutes for juices to settle. To serve, place 3 peach halves onto a serving plate, squeeze over a little of the lime juice along with any of the residual sauce from the baking dish and top with the fresh ricotta.

"blessed are the cheese makers"

monty python's life of brian.

Great Berrier Reef

Serves: 2

As we get older it's increasingly important to eat antioxidant rich food, for example oranges, blueberries, tea and tomatoes. I am a firm believer that prevention is better than cure, so filling our gas tanks with the right fuel is an element to living a healthy lifestyle.

1 fresh lime, cut in quarters
2 tbs palm sugar
½ cup fresh mint leaves
¾ cup blueberries
¾ cup raspberries
¾ cup strawberries
2 oranges, juiced
2 cups crushed ice

In a large jug, place the quarters of lime, palm sugar and mint leaves, along with the berries and proceed to crush with muddling stick (thick long stick) or the end of a rolling pin.

Crush until berries have turned to a pulp. Add orange juice along with the crushed ice, mix well and serve.

Tomatoes on Toast

As simple as this sounds, this is one of my favourite breakfast meals. Big fat juicy tomatoes warmed with a hint of fresh tarragon and garlic, served on a slab of toasted brioche. If the tomatoes are perfectly ripe then get set for the perfect weekend breakfast, along with the newspaper and a glass of fresh juice.

1 large Ox heart tomato, or 3 small vine ripened tomatoes

3 tbs (60ml/2 fl oz) extra virgin olive oil

1 tbs butter

2 sprigs fresh tarragon (or 1 tsp dried)

1 clove garlic, finely sliced

1 slice of Brioche or Italian Ciabatta

Serves: This recipe is per person

Note: This dish is always going to taste better when the tomatoes are at their ripest, when they are bursting with flavour and juice.

To prepare the tomatoes, remove the core using a small knife and plunge into a pot of boiling water for 20 to 30 seconds to help loosen skin. Remove from boiling water and plunge into ice cold water. Remove the skin.

Pat tomato dry with a paper towel, cut into thickish wedges and place into a smallish pan along with olive oil, butter, tarragon leaves and sliced garlic.

Place pan onto heat, cover and warm over a gentle heat for a few minutes until the tomatoes just start to break down, but still stay intact, approximately 5 to 7 minutes.

Serve the tomatoes on lightly toasted brioche, preferably grilled to give you the char markings and a wonderful smokey flavour (optional).

Croque Madame

Serves: 6

Note: Leftover filling will keep in the refrigerator for 3 days.

When frying eggs I always use a non-stick pan and cook over a moderate to low heat, so egg stays soft and not crisp around the edges.

I love toasted sandwiches. I have such fond memories of growing up and one particular memory was Sunday night dinner consisting of spaghetti and cheese toasted sandwiches, they were so good! I have given a recipe for something a little more sophisticated with the addition of fibre rich wholegrain bread. It doesn't matter what time of the day you eat this, it's a great snack, but more often than not it's an awesome weekend breakfast.

250gm (8 oz) grated Swiss cheese, at room temperature
Yolk of 1 large egg
1 tbs Worcestershire sauce
1 tbs smooth Dijon mustard
Pinch of cayenne pepper
Pinch of salt
200gm (7 oz) thinly sliced ham
¼ cup (60ml/2 fl oz) cream, if needed to thin the cheese mixture
12 slices home-made style wholegrain bread
Olive oil, for frying
6 eggs

Put the cheese, egg yolk, Worcestershire sauce, mustard and cayenne in a food processor fitted with a metal blade and process until smooth. Taste and adjust seasoning with salt if needed, remembering the ham will contribute to the saltiness.

If the mixture is too thick to spread, thin out with a little of the cream. Spread the cheese mixture over one side of each bread slice. Arrange ham over the cheese on half of the slices of bread and invert the remaining bread over the ham. Press the sandwich firmly together.

Pour a little oil into the bottom of a heavy skillet and heat it over a medium-high heat until hot. Fry sandwich until golden and crisp on both sides. Repeat with remaining sandwiches.

To serve, top each sandwich with a lightly fried egg, sunny side up.

Scrambled Eggs with Asparagus

They say the best scrambled eggs are the ones with the most fat in them, well try these babies. I've replaced the cream with a flavoursome extra virgin olive oil. Not only have we substituted a saturated fat for a polyunsaturated fat, but they taste damn good too.

I love the look of the asparagus stems being partially peeled, a little more time consuming but visually worth the effort! Feel free to substitute asparagus for tomatoes, mushrooms or spinach cooked to your liking.

2 (60gm/2 oz) eggs

2 tbs (40ml/1⅓rd fl oz) extra virgin olive oil

Pinch of salt and ground pepper, preferably white

Pinch of ground nutmeg

½ tsp butter

5 spears of asparagus, blanched until tender and base partly peeled

1 slice of ciabatta, toasted or your favourite bread (waxy Italian bread)

Using a fork lightly beat the eggs, oil and seasoning together. Melt the butter in a non-stick pan over a medium low heat. Pour in the eggs, allowing to partially set before using a wooden spoon to pull the eggs back as you tilt the pan forward. The trick here is to be as gentle as possible trying not to work the eggs too much.

Repeat the process of pulling the spoon through the eggs till almost set, should only take a couple of minutes. Once set, remove from pan ASAP to stop further cooking and drying out. Serve eggs with asparagus and toasted ciabatta.

Serves: This recipe is per person

Note: Treat thy pan with love, so no harsh scrubbing and scraping and it will bear you perfect eggs every time.

Almond and Honey Frappe

Serves: 2

I'm not sure which part of this drink I love most, the creamy almond flavour with a hint of honey or the feeling of squeezing almonds and milk through muslin cloth.

Your skin will thank you for it and your taste buds will be begging for more, it truly is worth the effort.

400g (14 oz) blanched almonds (skins removed)
1 cup (250ml/8 fl oz) milk
70g (2½ oz) honey
1½ cups ice

Place the almonds in a blender with the milk and 100mls (3¼ fl oz) of water and process to a fine paste.

Transfer to a large, double thickness of muslin cloth, pulling the corners in and then twisting to make a tight ball. Squeeze over a bowl to collect the almond milk.

Place the almond milk along with honey and ice in a clean blender, blend till smooth then serve.

Love my snacks. I am a huge advocate for eating smaller meals more often, in fact I am a compulsive grazer. I do my best to make snacking as wholesome as possible whether it's a simple piece of fruit or a delicious chicken chimmichanga.

Snacking is one of the essential elements to a full and active day. Snacks will help sustain energy levels, hasten metabolism and heighten concentration.

I generally carry around with me a little bag of nuts, a piece of fruit or a few energy balls for instant access. And when I'm getting together with friends I'll make an effort to put together a few chicken sandwiches or roast some delicious macadamia nuts.

Most of the snacks in this section rely upon basic pantry elements with a few fresh elements thrown in for good measure.

Hey trust me, snacking is the new black.

snackelements

3 Foot Chicken Sandwich

Serves: 10

Note: If you are off on a day trip or to a picnic, ensure that the sandwich is transported in a cooler or Eski.

Here's a great sandwich option that will feed about 10 for lunch easily at a picnic or BBQ. Whatever the occasion it always looks impressive, tastes great and is simple to make. I have recipes for roasting a chicken and mayonnaise in the book, but feel free for convenience sake to just buy them already done. This will take a good hour of preparation out of it.

1 baguette, approximately 3 foot long

1 cup (250ml/8fl oz) mayonnaise

1 tbs lemon juice

1 tsp paprika

Salt and freshly ground black pepper

1 whole roasted chicken, bones and skin discarded and flesh roughly chopped

See page 174 for roast chicken recipe

2 stalks celery, trimmed, peeled and finely diced

½ cup (80g/3oz) toasted almonds, roughly chopped

3 tbs chopped flat leaf parsley

Cut lengthwise along the side of the baguette with a bread knife but don't cut all the way through. Open it up and hollow it out. (Freeze the fresh bread taken from inside as they make wicked breadcrumbs).*

Mix the mayonnaise with the lemon juice and season with paprika, salt and pepper. Fold through the chopped chicken, celery, almonds and chopped parsley then stuff into the hollowed baguette.

For presentation, I like to tie the baguette with string and then cut into individual portions. Wrapped in plastic wrap, this will keep in the fridge for a few hours, but is definitely best served fresh.

*Great to use in stuffed artichokes on page 133 or lasagne with crab and tomato on page 146.

Fried Olives

Lucky these are easy to make because they are addictive if you love olives! This is a great dish on its own or perfect to serve on an antipasto platter.

Serves: 6

400g (14 oz) mixed olives (cleared of any salt or brine and not stuffed)
1 tbs (20ml/½ fl oz) olive oil
1 clove garlic, crushed

¼ cup (60ml/2 fl oz) balsamic vinegar
1 tbs chopped marjoram or oregano
1 birdseye chilli, finely sliced

Lightly fry the olives in the olive oil with the garlic for a few minutes. Add the vinegar and simmer until nearly evaporated. Add the chilli, marjoram or oregano. Cook for a further minute and serve piping hot.

* green Sicilian, Kalamata and wild olives were used in the shot of this recipe.

Radish and Fennel with Sea Salt

We all know how good raw vegetables are for us, but did you know they can taste really delicious too? This is a perfect dish on its own, or great to add to an antipasto platter.

Serves: 4

8 radishes, washed and tops trimmed
1 medium sized fennel bulb
2 tbs (40ml/1 fl oz) lemon juice

Extra virgin olive oil
Sea salt to taste and freshly ground black pepper, to taste

Score the tops of each radish with a cross about 5mm/¼ inch deep.

Slice the fennel into 5mm/¼ inch thick slices and douse with the lemon juice.

Pour a thin layer of olive oil onto a serving plate, season with sea salt flakes and coarsely ground black pepper.

Stand the radishes in the olive oil and arrange the fennel onto the same plate. Serve.

Li'l Burgers

Serves: 12 children's size or 6 adult size

NOTE: It is important to remember when preparing any minced meat that everything that is used is not just clean but also well chilled, not just ingredients but equipment as well.

Theses are a great snack idea, perfect for kids parties and so easy to eat.

The burger patties can be prepared the day before, but certainly should be cooked through.

500gm (1.1lb) lean beef mince
½ tsp Dijon mustard
1 tbs Worcestershire sauce
1 carrot, grated
1 zucchini, grated (courgette)
2 tbs chopped parsley
2 tbs tomato sauce/ketchup
1 egg
½ cup breadcrumbs
Pinch of salt

12 mini burger buns or muffins lightly toasted
1 small iceberg or romaine lettuce, finely shredded
2 tomatoes, thinly sliced
1 x 225g (½ lb) can sliced beetroot, well drained
Tomato sauce/ketchup to serve

Mix the beef mince, mustard, Worcestershire sauce, carrot, zucchini, parsley, tomato sauce, egg and breadcrumbs. Season with salt and pepper. Measure out rough portions of about 70g/2½ oz) and mould into burger patties. Refrigerate immediately.

To cook, place little flattened patties into a hot pan with a little olive oil. Fry until golden on both sides. Repeat with remaining patties until all are cooked. Burgers could also be cooked on the BBQ.

Build your burgers with remaining ingredients. I like to start with the base of the bun topped with lettuce, beef patty, followed by tomato, beetroot and then tomato sauce/ketchup. Top with the lid and serve.

Ricotta and Asparagus Wraps

Here's a great little number to tempt the taste buds. Now I love anchovies so I would be inclined to add more than the quantity below however I've only added a couple to this recipe. You'll get a slight salty hit and it won't be offensive, trust me.

This wrap also doubles as finger food, just slice the golden roll into 2cm lengths and serve as an appetiser, doused in a little extra virgin olive oil.

3 anchovy fillets*
½ clove garlic
120g (4 oz) fresh ricotta
3 tbs (60ml/2 fl oz) olive oil
Pinch of salt and freshly ground black pepper, to taste
2 large flour tortilla's
4 to 6 spears of asparagus

Serves: 2

* If using whole anchovies packed in salt, after removing them from the packaging, brush excess salt off and remove backbone using fingers.

48

Finely chop the anchovies and garlic together until you've almost created a paste, throw into a bowl along with the ricotta, 1 tablespoon (20ml/½ fl oz) of the olive oil, salt and pepper and give a good mix.

Spread evenly over the tortilla, leaving a 3cm/1 inch strip along the longer side of the tortilla uncovered.

Blanch the asparagus in boiling water for 4 to 5 minutes until tender then refresh under cold running water. Dry them well. Place the asparagus down the centre of the ricotta and then roll the tortilla up firmly.

Heat the remaining olive oil in a pan over a medium heat, place the roll into the pan, flap side down, turning every 20 to 30 seconds to get an even golden colour.

To serve, cut into small pieces. Definitely best eaten hot straight out of the pan.

Chicken and Pearl Barley Soup

Serves: 10 hearty portions

Note: If the soup is looking a little dry just feed it water.

It will freeze however it will certainly lose some of its goodness.

Using a whole chicken allows for the goodness that is derived from the bones.

Will keep in the refrigerator for
5 days.

Feeling a little under the weather? I strongly recommend a helping or two of piping hot chicken and pearl barley soup to ward off any colds and flu symptoms. Not only is it medicinal, it's absolutely delicious. I suggest using organic chicken and organic vegetables whenever possible.

1 whole organic chicken, about a size 12 (about 1.2kg/2.6lb)

3 tbs (60m/½ fl oz) olive oil

2 onions, finely chopped

7 cloves of garlic

2 sprigs of fresh rosemary (dried)

1 extra large knob of ginger, peeled and finely chopped

500g (1.1lb) packet of pearl barley

2 medium sized carrots, skin on and finely chopped

5 stalks of celery, finely chopped

2 litres (3½ pints) chicken stock

½ bunch parsley, chopped

Salt and freshly ground black pepper

Choose a heavy based saucepan large enough to take the whole chicken. Heat olive oil and add onions, garlic, rosemary and ginger. Stir for 2 to 3 minutes until softened and fragrant.

Add the pearl barley, carrots and celery. Place the chicken on top and cover with chicken stock and enough water to submerge the chicken.

Bring to the boil and simmer for about 25 to 30 minutes (depending on the size of the chicken) and then turn of and allow to cool naturally. When cool remove chicken. Pull the chicken apart using your hands and discard both the skin and bones. Finely chop or feather the chicken meat and fold through the soup, along with parsley. Season with a little salt and pepper to taste.

Roasted Macadamia Nuts with Garlic and Fennel Seed

This is an addictive little snack that doubles nicely as pre dinner nibblies.
If macadamias are not available or to your liking, try whole almonds, hazelnuts or even Brazil nuts.

3 tbs (60ml/2 fl oz) olive oil

3 cloves garlic, thinly sliced

1 tbs fennel seeds

¼ tsp chilli flakes

250g (9 oz) shelled macadamia nuts

Salt and freshly ground black pepper, to taste

Place the oil in a heavy based pan over a medium heat; add the garlic, fennel seeds, chilli flakes and the nuts. Turn the nuts frequently, being careful not to burn the garlic.

When golden and fragrant (approximately 3 minutes), drain well on absorbent paper, season with salt and pepper, serve whilst warm.

Providing well drained of oil, nuts will keep in sealed, airtight container for 4 to 6 days.

Serves: 5 to 6

Note: For those of you who are not partial to chilli and garlic, this method can also be used for plain roasted nuts, just add salt to taste.

52

Tuna and White Bean Puree

Serves: 5 to 6

This has the texture of a pate and a flavour worthy of seconds.
A good dip for all occasions and will cost you peanuts to make.

200g (7 oz) can tuna, drained

400g (14 oz) can cannellini beans, drained

⅓ cup (80ml/2½ fl oz) extra virgin olive oil

1 garlic clove, finely chopped

Pinch of salt and lashings of ground black pepper

1 loaf of Ciabatta or baguette, toasted for serving

Place drained tuna, cannellini beans, olive oil and garlic into a food processor and blend to a smooth paste. Add seasoning to taste. Serve with dry toast and salad.

Puree will keep for a good 2 to 3 days in the refrigerator if covered with a thin layer of olive oil.

Almost an Aussie Meat Pie

Serves: 4

Note: This is a great 'prepare ahead' dish where you can have everything done up to putting it into the oven. You can be a good day ahead with the pies sitting in the fridge. Important to remember though that if the pie filling has come straight from the fridge it will take a little longer to heat in the oven.

Aah the famous Aussie meat pie. For my international readers, a pie is a minced/ground beef and gravy filling encased in pastry.

Nothing beats watching a great game of AFL, Rugby League or Cricket and eating this famous Australian food. There is nothing in the world quite like a pie, it's as synonymous with Australia as kangaroos, Holden cars, the Sydney Opera House and the Harbour Bridge.

Here is a "take" on the humble Aussie pie to give you a taste of what all the fuss is about!

1 onion, finely chopped

500g (1.1lb) lean beef mince

3 tbs (50g/1¾ oz) plain flour

1 cup (250ml/8fl oz) beef stock

¼ cup (60ml/2 fl oz) tomato sauce (ketchup)

2 tsp Worcestershire sauce

Sea salt and freshly ground black pepper

½ tsp dried oregano

Pinch of nutmeg

1 sheet ready rolled puff pastry

1 beaten egg, for glazing

In a medium sized pan, cook both the onion and mince until well browned. Sprinkle over the flour, mixing well to incorporate. Add stock in 3 batches, stirring well between each.

Add the tomato and Worcestershire sauces. Bring to the boil then lower the heat to a simmer and cook for a further five minutes stirring frequently.

Season with a good pinch of salt, a good grinding of black pepper and oregano. Remove from heat and allow to sit for 15 minutes.

Pre heat oven to 230°C/450°F. Choose your desired dish* and invert over pastry. Cut pastry rounds allowing an extra 2cm/⅘th inch larger than the top of the dish. Fill the dish with meat mixture leaving a little space from the top.

Brush rim of pie dish with beaten egg, lightly press pastry round on top and brush with egg. Bake 15 to 20 minutes, until pastry is well risen. Serve with extra tomato sauce (ketchup).

* I suggest either 4 individual coffee cups for individual pies, or a medium sized pie tin.

55

Almond and Apricot Energy Balls

I love my energy balls! They are really easy to make and you can play around with different nuts and dried fruits once you get the hang of this. The idea is that you always have some sort of snack available when you're craving something sweet. At least with these, you know it's not full of artificial sweeteners and preservatives, and they taste so good. Don't eat all 30 at once though, it's nice to share!

1 cup (90g/3oz) rolled oats
1 cup (150g/5oz) dried apricots
1 cup (90g/3oz) dried apple
1 cup (160g/5½ oz) pitted dates
½ cup (160g/5½ oz) chopped almonds
½ cup (170g/5½ oz) raisins
2 dried figs, chopped
½ cup (125ml/4 fl oz) orange juice
30g (1oz) black sesame seeds or shredded coconut

Mix all ingredients, (except orange juice and sesame seeds) together in a large bowl. Process mixture in 3 separate batches in a food processor with enough orange juice until mixture sticks together.

Roll mixture into small balls and roll in black sesame seeds (or coconut) to coat. Place into an airtight container and refrigerate overnight to firm. Will keep refrigerated for up to a week.

Serves: 30 balls

"Never eat more than you can lift". miss piggy

Tomato and Goats Cheese Tart

Serves: 8

Damien's Flaky Pastry

260g (9 oz) plain flour

180g (6½ oz) chilled butter

Pinch salt

50ml (1½ fl oz) water

1 egg white

Zest of ½ a lemon (optional)

Pinch of cayenne pepper (optional)

Filling

3 x 60g (2 oz) eggs

450ml (14½ fl oz) cream

Pinch white pepper

Pinch nutmeg

50g (1¾ oz) firm goats cheese

2 vine ripened tomatoes – oven dried (see note)

I have given a recipe for the most incredibly textured pastry I have ever eaten. This is a recipe handed down by my mentor Damien Pignolet, who has been a colleague and good friend for many years. Feel free to use a commercial brand for convenience, just remember to cook the pastry till it's crisp, you'll end up with a much better product.

Sift the flour and salt on to a clean bench or flat surface. Grate the butter over the flour. Using your hands lightly lift the flour through the butter separating all the little clusters, coating butter evenly with flour and pour on the water. Using the heel of your hand proceed by pushing the butter into the flour away from yourself. Pull flour and butter back and repeat till flour has absorbed the butter and you are left with dough. Wrap the dough tightly in plastic wrap and rest* in the refrigerator for an hour before using.

Pre-heat oven to 170°C/340°F. Roll out the pastry on a floured surface until it is 4mm/⅕th inch thick. Press into a round 23 to 27cm (9 to 10½ inch) tart tin and rest in the refrigerator for 10 minutes. Cover the pastry with a piece of parchment paper or lightly buttered aluminium foil and fill with blind baking weights, dried pulses or rice.

Blind bake in the oven for approximately 20 to 25 minutes then remove foil and weights, return to oven for about 5 minutes to finish browning. Brush the hot pastry shell with lightly beaten egg white, to seal any possible cracks, dry in oven for a further 2 minutes.

Place eggs, cream, white pepper and nutmeg into a medium sized bowl and beat lightly with a fork until well mixed but not aerated (no bubbles). Once all ingredients are mixed, set the bowl over a pot of lightly simmering water, mixing constantly for 2 to 3 minutes until mixture is lukewarm, but not hot.

Carefully pour custard into the prepared tart shell, drop oven temperature to 125°C and bake for 30 minutes. Remove tart and place the goats cheese and tomato on top. Return to the oven for a further 5 minutes. When cooked, the custard filling should still have a slight wobble to it, but not be runny. Allow to cool before serving. Best eaten within the day.

See next page for photographs of method.

Note: To oven dry tomatoes, slice 5mm/⅕th inch thick and sprinkle with dried thyme leaves and black pepper and cook at 155°C/310°F for 2 hours.

* Resting is a process that allows the gluten in the flour to relax and minimise shrinking whilst cooking.

damien's
flaky pastry

tomato and goats
cheese tart

Zucchini (Courgette) and Feta Omelette with Fresh Mint

Omelettes make great quick snacks, don't think just breakfast.

Serves: 1

1 small zucchini (courgette)
2 tsp olive oil
2 eggs
½ egg shell of water (approx 2 tablespoons)
Salt and freshly ground black pepper, to taste
30g (1 oz) firm feta cheese
Fresh mint leaves (or Basil or Arugula)

Cut the zucchini (courgette) into small dice. Lightly sauté in a small non-stick pan using 1 teaspoon of the olive oil. Cook until lightly golden in colour, remove from pan and set aside.

Beat eggs and water lightly with a fork and season with salt and pepper. Add remaining olive oil to the pan, then eggs, and cook over medium heat, lifting the side of the omelette and tilting the pan to let the uncooked eggs run out to the edges.

When omelette is seconds from being set, scatter over the zucchini, feta and a little fresh mint. To serve, turn the omelette out of the pan lifting the sides inwards and folding as you flip out.

"one of the very nicest things about life is the way we must regularly stop whatever it is we are doing and devote our attention to eating". Luciano Pavarotti and William Wright, Pavarotti, my own story

Roasted Corn and Black Bean Cones

Serves: 12 small portions

Note: *Feel free to roast your own capsicum (peppers), I do have a recipe on page 267 that shows you how to do it. For the sake of convenience, feel free to use pre-roasted capsicums (peppers).

#For dry beans, soak for 7 hours, preferably overnight in the refrigerator. Drain and cover with fresh water, adding a sprig of fresh rosemary, ⅓ cup olive oil and bring to a boil and simmer for 40 minutes, or until tender.

This is a great little party snack I came up with for a show called *"You're Invited"*™ on the *"E"* network in America. It's perfect outside food as it can get a little drippy.

2 cobs of fresh corn

1 tbs (20ml/½ fl oz) olive oil

2 whole roasted capsicums/bell peppers, finely chopped*

400g (14 oz) can black beans, well drained#

½ bunch of coriander/cilantro leaves, chopped

Salt and freshly ground black pepper, to taste

12 flour tortillas, approximately 20cm/8 inch in diameter

Extra olive oil for brushing

basil mayonnaise – see page 86

65

Remove corn kernels from the cob by laying cob on a chopping board and using a sharp knife, cut away shards of corn kernels.

Place kernels into pan with olive oil and sauté over a medium heat until golden. Fold through roasted capsicum, beans and coriander and season to taste.

Brush both sides of each tortilla with olive oil then lightly toast each side over the a char grill or griddle pan. Remove from heat, fold in half and then in half again to create a cone like pocket.

Fill cone with the corn salsa, finishing with a small dollop of basil mayonnaise before serving.

Saffron and Corn Soup

I have served this soup on a number of occasions and will always have at least one person asking for more. It is quite rich, so I will generally serve it as a little starter, either in a shot glass or a little short black cup with saucer.

3 cobs of fresh corn

1 tbs (20g/¾ oz) butter

2 tbs (40ml/1 fl oz) olive oil

1 medium sized leek, white part only, finely chopped

1 large potato, preferably a Desiree, peeled and finely diced

3 tbs flour

1 big pinch of saffron

3 cups (750ml/24 fl oz) boiling chicken stock*

½ cup (125ml/4 fl oz) cream

Salt and freshly ground black pepper, to taste

I find the easiest way to remove corn kernels from the cob is to hold the whole cob (skin and silk removed) flat down on a chopping board and using a chefs knife, cut away the corn in large shards, rolling the corn as you go.

In a heavy based saucepan over a medium heat, melt the butter with the olive oil. Add corn, leek and potato and sweat for a few minutes. Sprinkle over the flour, mixing well to stop flour clumping. Lower the heat and cook for a couple of minutes before gradually adding the boiling chicken stock, mixing well between each addition. Add the saffron and cook for 15 to 20 minutes until potato is soft.

Transfer to a blender and puree until smooth. Pass through a sieve and then return to the saucepan. Add cream, bring to the boil and season with salt and pepper.

To serve pour into desired vessel and top with a little fresh cream, extra virgin olive oil and cracked black pepper.

*Vegetable stock can also be used.

66

Lamb Pan Pizza

Serves: 8 slices

I have always been inspired by the classic apple Tarte Tatin, this dish may be a savoury pizza but it is certainly a reflection on how the Tatin sisters made their tart.

1 sheet butter puff pastry
1 small Spanish (red) onion, finely diced
2 tbs (40ml/1 fl oz) olive oil
½ tsp ground cumin
½ tsp ground coriander
¼ tsp ground cloves
350g (12 oz) minced/ground lamb
1 tomato, finely chopped
2 tbs HP sauce*
½ cup (125ml/4 fl oz) chicken stock

¼ cup chopped parsley
½ cup finely shredded red cabbage or white cabbage if unavailable

Yoghurt dressing

2 tbs natural yoghurt
2 tbs extra virgin olive oil
6 leaves of fresh mint
Pinch of Salt and freshly ground black pepper

Preheat oven to 230°C/450°F. Choose a non-stick pan about 25 to 30cm (10 to 12 inches) in diameter, with an oven proof handle. Invert the pan over the sheet of puff pastry and cut around it, giving you a perfect fitting lid. Refrigerate until needed.

Place pan over a moderate heat and sweat the onions in the olive oil until translucent, approximately 5 minutes. Add the spices and cook for a further 30 seconds before adding the minced lamb. Cook the lamb until lightly browned, then add tomato, HP sauce and chicken stock and cook until moisture has pretty much evaporated. Mix in the chopped parsley.

Place the sheet of pastry over the minced lamb and put straight into the oven. Cook for approximately 10 to 12 minutes, until pastry is well risen and golden brown.

Meanwhile, combine dressing ingredients together. Cool pizza for 3 minutes before inverting onto a serving dish. Scatter with shredded cabbage and drizzle with the yoghurt and mint dressing.

Note: If HP sauce is unavailable, use 1 tbs of tomato sauce/ketchup with 1 tsp of Worcestershire sauce

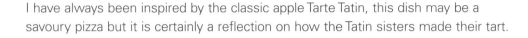

Tapenade

I am aware that most convenience stores/supermarkets will stock some sort of olive paste, tapenade these days, but I guarantee they don't compare to the freshness of making your own. Once you've made this recipe, store it, covered with a couple of tablespoons of olive oil in an air tight container in the fridge for up to 2 weeks.

250g (9 oz) pitted kalamata olives
2 roasted red capsicums (bell peppers)*, blackened skin and seeds removed
5 anchovies
2 cloves garlic
⅓ cup flat leaf parsley
3 tbs (60ml/2 fl oz) olive oil
1 tbs capers
1 tbs balsamic vinegar
Pepper to taste

Puree all ingredients together to form a smooth paste, using pepper to give a bite.

*For roasting capsicums/bell peppers see page 267.

Makes: 2 cups

Note: For a variation try using green olives

Chicken Chimmichanga (Mexican)

Here's another quick and easy recipe that I love making at home, originally deep fried served with sour cream and mozzarella, I have modified it to reduce saturated fat content, served as a meal or as a snack is entirely up to you, enjoy.

1 tbs (20ml/½ fl oz) olive oil

1 Spanish (red) onion, finely chopped

2 cloves garlic, chopped

1 tsp ground cumin

½ tsp ground allspice

½ tsp chilli flakes

500g (1.1lb) chicken mince

400g (14oz) can crushed tomatoes

2 tbs fresh coriander (cilantro) leaves, chopped

6 flour tortillas

1 cup (100g/3½ oz) grated mozzarella, (low fat, if available)

2 tbs (40ml/1 fl oz) olive oil, extra

1 avocado

½ cup (120g/4½ oz) low fat sour cream, optional

Heat oil in a frying pan. Cook onion and garlic until soft. Add spices and cook for a further 30 to 40 seconds.

Add the chicken mince, and cook until meat has browned. Add tomatoes and simmer for 5 minutes, if looking a little dry add a little water to moisten. Stir through the coriander (cilantro) and set aside to cool.

Place mixture down the centre of the tortillas, sprinkle with grated cheese, tuck in the sides and roll up.

Heat the extra oil up in a frying pan. Place the parcel in the pan, seam side down. Cook on a low heat until golden. Turn and cook on all sides until crisp.

To serve, cut in half, serve with wedges of avocado, a scoop of the sour cream and maybe topped with a few extra coriander (cilantro) leaves.

Eggplant Caviar

This is a great little snack served with crusty bread or as an accompaniment to a piece of BBQ'd fish.

Serves: 8 as a snack or 4 side portions

2 large eggplants/aubergines

1 small Spanish (red) onion, finely diced

1 capsicum (bell pepper), seeds and pith removed, finely diced

1 small red chilli, seeds removed and finely chopped

1 tsp ground coriander (cilantro) seeds

¼ cup (60ml/2 fl oz) extra virgin olive oil

Juice of one lime

3 tbs chopped coriander/cilantro

Salt and freshly ground black pepper, to taste

Roast the whole eggplant over a hot griddle pan or BBQ until soft and blackened. This should take a good 10 to 15 minutes. Place into a bowl and cover with plastic wrap or a towel allowing eggplant to cool and sweat.

Once cooled, carefully remove the blackened skin (never rinse under water as this will wash away flavour). Cut the flesh into a rough dice, no need to be too precise.

Carefully mix remaining ingredients together and combine with eggplant, adding a little salt and pepper to taste.

"how can people say they don't eat eggplant when god loves the color and the french love the name? I don't understand." Jeff Smith, The Frugal Gourmet

Tomato and Chorizo Soup

Serves: 4

It's the chorizo sausage in this soup that makes it so special, the flavour is incredible for such a simple dish.

Chorizo is a highly textured Spanish sausage filled with garlic, chilli and other spices, and the risoni is rice shaped pasta that adds a refined texture to this simple peasant style dish. Feel free however to use any other small pasta as a substitute if risoni is not available.

2 tbs olive oil
1 chorizo sausage, skin removed and cut into small cubes
1 small onion, finely chopped
2 cloves garlic, chopped
420g (15 oz) can crushed tomatoes
1.5 litres (48 fl oz) chicken stock
1 cup (220g/7¾ oz) risoni, broken spaghetti or small pasta shells
3 cups shredded silverbeet or spinach
1 cup (120g/4 oz) frozen peas
Salt and freshly ground black pepper, to taste

Heat olive oil in a large heavy based pan, Add chorizo sausage and brown over a medium heat, allowing some of the fat to render away, when evenly coloured, drain off any excess fat.

Add onion and garlic and cook for a further 30 seconds. Add tomatoes and stock and bring to the boil. Reduce the heat and add the risoni. Simmer for 5 minutes or until nearly tender.

Stir through spinach and peas and cook for a further 2 minutes. Season with salt and pepper and serve.

Spanish Tortilla with Green Olives

This dish is perfect served with a salad of watercress, chervil and basil, dressed with olive oil and balsamic vinegar.

Serves: 6

150ml (5 fl oz) olive oil
500g (1.1 lb) potatoes, thinly sliced*
1 large onion, sliced
1 clove garlic, crushed
6 eggs
1 tbs fresh or dried thyme
Salt and freshly ground black pepper, to taste
10 green olives, seeds removed and finely chopped

Heat ⅓ cup (80ml/2.5 fl oz) of the olive oil in a non-stick pan over medium heat till hot. Reduce temperature to low then add the potatoes, onion and garlic stirring frequently for 10 to 15 minutes or until potatoes are tender. Remove from heat and cool slightly.

Beat the eggs in a large bowl with thyme, salt and pepper. Stir in the olives. Using a slotted spoon, transfer the potatoes and onion to the egg mixture, discarding any excess oil.

Return pan to heat and add 2 tablespoons of the olive oil. Pour in the potato mixture and arrange potatoes and onions in the bottom of the pan. Cook for about 8 minutes, shaking the pan occasionally, until set.

Loosen the tortilla with a spatula and place a large plate over the pan. Invert the tortilla onto the plate. Add remaining oil to the pan and slide uncooked side of the tortilla into the pan. Push down sides of the tortilla with a spatula and continue to cook for a further 3 to 5 minutes.

Remove from the pan and allow to cool for 10 minutes before cutting.

* Potatoes can be sliced either by hand or with a mandolin which will give a more consistent size to the slices.

Pickled Cherries

Note: Discard any bruised or bad cherries as these could send an entire jar bad.

It almost seems senseless to pickle cherries, especially when they're big fat, super sweet, juicy and in season. Yum! I eat them for breakfast, lunch and dinner.

Why would you bother pickling them? Here's why. To have them when they're not in season is why. Serving these alongside any cold meat or paté is an absolute treat. I have been known to give the occasional jar of pickled cherries as a gift. You need a months minimum pickling time before eating, not a day earlier. They will keep for good year if stored in a cool place in a sterilised jar.

2.5 litres (4⅓ pints) white wine vinegar

1.25 kg (2¾ lb) brown sugar

15 cloves

15 juniper berries (optional)

2 lemons, zest thinly stripped, juice not needed

3 cinnamon sticks

2.5 kg (5½ lb) fresh cherries, stems trimmed to half length

Place all ingredients except cherries in a large pan. Stir to dissolve the sugar and slowly bring to the boil. Reduce heat and simmer for 10 minutes. Remove from heat and allow to cool, preferably overnight.

Place prepared cherries into sterilised jars.* Pour over cool pickling liquid and seal. Cherries will need to sit for a good month before eating.

* To sterilise jars and lids, carefully submerge in a pot of boiling water for 10 to 15 seconds, remove with
a pair of tongs and set to cool with opening of the jar facing down, set over a towel. Allow jar to cool before filling.

Jerusalem Artichokes with Crème Fraiche and Salmon Pearls

When shopping for Jerusalem artichokes, try and find similar sized ones, so they cook evenly. Don't be put off by all the butter; you discard most of it after cooking.

Serves: 4 as an appetiser

4 small Jerusalem artichokes (golf ball size), scrubbed

100g (3½ oz) butter

½ cup (125ml/4 fl oz) olive oil

1 clove garlic, bruised

3 sprigs thyme (or ½ tsp dried)

Salt and freshly ground black pepper, to taste

4 tsp crème fraiche or sour cream

2 tbs salmon eggs, to garnish or caviar found in refrigerated section of specialty deli's or food stores.

Chervil to garnish

Place the artichokes in a small ovenproof dish with butter, olive oil, garlic, thyme and seasoning. Cover with foil and place in an oven at 190°C/375°F for approximately 40 to 50 minutes, until soft to touch (times will vary depending on artichokes).

Allow artichokes to cool slightly, remove from butter and drain. Score the top of each artichoke with a sharp knife to make an opening.

On each artichoke place a spoon of crème fraiche, a small amount of the salmon eggs, garnish with chervil and cracked black pepper.

Capsicum (Bell Pepper) Relish

Two words for you, "SAUSAGES & BURGERS".

With the quantity of vinegar and sugar in this recipe, it will certainly keep for a long period of time. It is so delicious, and friends and family will envy you for it. It gives that little extra zing to old favourites.

2 Spanish (red) onions, finely chopped

50ml (1½ fl oz) olive oil

1kg (2.2 lb) red capsicum/bell pepper cut into 1cm squares

1 clove garlic, finely chopped

1 tsp ground ginger

½ tsp allspice

120g (4oz) brown sugar

240ml (8fl oz) white wine vinegar

100g (3½ oz) sultanas soaked in 80ml (2½ fl oz) Verjuice* for an hour

500g (1.1 lb) tomatoes, peeled, deseeded and chopped, for convenience, canned tomatoes will be fine

Sweat the onions in the olive oil until softened. Add the chopped capsicum and cook, covered for a further 5 minutes over a medium low heat. When capsicum has wilted, add the garlic, ginger, allspice, brown sugar, vinegar and soaked sultanas. Mix well then add the tomatoes, being careful not to break them up too much. Allow to slowly simmer for 40 minutes, stirring occasionally. The consistency should be thick and homogenous rather than watery. Will need to be bottled hot in sterilised jars#.

*Verjuice; unfermented green grape juice, apple juice could be used as a substitute.

#For information on sterilising jars, see Pickled Cherries recipe on page 81.

Basic Mayonnaise

I've always believed food that you make yourself, starting from scratch, will always taste better than any store bought product, no matter how good a cook you are. Practice makes perfect.

A fresh mayonnaise made with a beautiful olive oil and a flavouring of choice can really be a tantalising experience.

1 egg yolk

1 tsp smooth Dijon mustard

1 tbs lemon juice

Pinch of salt

1 cup (250ml/8 fl oz) olive oil

Pepper, to taste

In a bowl mix together the egg yolk, mustard, lemon juice and salt.

In a fine stream, pour olive oil whisking at the same time to create an emulsion of all ingredients.

If mayonnaise tastes a little oily on the palate, add a touch more lemon juice, on the other hand if it tastes a little too tart then add a little more olive oil. Season with pepper and serve.

Mayonnaise varieties

Basil Mayonnaise – to the basic mayonnasie recipe, add ¼ cup finely shredded basic leaves.

Smokey Mayonnaise – to the basic recipe, add 1½ tsp hot smoked paprika and a tablespoon of chopped parsley.

Fine Herb Mayonnaise – to the basic mayonaise recipe, add 1 tbs finely chopped chervil, chives, tarragon and parsley.

Lime Mayonnaise – in the basic mayonnaise recipe, add lime juice instead of lemon juice and also the zest of 1 lime.

Aioli – place 5 cloves of garlic in a small pan covered with water and bring to the boil. When boiled, strain garlic and cover with fresh cold water and bring to the boil again, this time simmering for 5 minutes, or until soft. When cool, push garlic out of its skin, crush in a mortar and pestle along with a pinch of salt. When smooth, mix into the basic mayonnaise.

Serves: Makes 1½ cups

TIPS FOR MAKING MAYO

Try to have all ingredients at the same temperature.

It's very important that any oil added is added slowly to omit seperation.

If your mayo splits, start again with an egg yolk, mustard and lemon juice, mix well and begin to pour in the split mayo in a fine stream.

Once you have mastered a basic mayonnaise recipe, try playing with different herbs and spices, it's fun.

Mayonnaise will keep in the refrigerator for 3 days.

Avocado Salsa

Serves: 2

How tasty, a thick piece of bread with a slathering of avocado salsa. Simple, delicious and very easy to make. Always nice alongside a selection of cold meats or seafood as well.

1 large avocado, firm but ripe

1 red capsicum (pepper), finely diced

3 tbs (60m½ fl oz) olive oil

Juice of 1 lime

1 birds eye chilli, seeds removed and finely chopped, or ¼ tsp dried chilli

½ bunch coriander (cilantro), finely chopped

Salt and freshly ground black pepper, to taste

1 Baguette/French stick

Olive oil

Extra coriander leaves for garnish

To remove avocado from flesh, split in half lengthways remembering there is a large seed inside. Remove seed and discard. Using a large spoon carefully remove flesh from skin using the spoon as a lever. Once flesh is removed, finely dice avocado into small cubes.

Add capsicum, olive oil, lime juice, chilli, coriander and enough salt and pepper to balance taste, remembering not to over mix. A coarse texture looks a little more presentable.

Take thickish slices of baguette, brush with olive oil and grill until lightly toasted on both sides. Spread avocado over the toasted baguette. Garnish with extra coriander leaves if desired.

As a child, I took so much pride in my little garden patch behind the chook pen on the farm. I would run home after getting off the school bus to water it and check if there were any signs of a new flower or bud, or if the birds had feasted on my labour during the day.

I grew zucchini, squash, watermelons and tomatoes. I remember being as happy as a pig in mud eating anything I grew. For a six or 7 year old, it was a treat and a real sense of achievement.

Nowadays, I rely upon the fruit and vegetable markets to inspire me, which they constantly do. I love seeing anything new—trying a new fruit or vegetable for the first time is always exciting.

I tend now to cook most of my garden elements using a low moisture method, where the fruit or vegetable retains its integrity and keeps what nature intended. You'll find out how to do this in this chapter.

After all, fruit and vegetables are packed with phytonutrients and phytochemicals, so beneficial to our everyday life and function.

gardenelements

Fennel, Orange and Olive Salad

Serves: 2

1 small fennel bulb
1 orange, skin removed and sliced into thin rounds
1 head of red endive
1 tsp olive oil
1 tsp white wine vinegar
½ tsp Dijon mustard
1 tbs light cream
1 tsp chopped parsley
Cracked black pepper
½ cup small wild/Ligurian olives

Remove the fennel tops and set aside. Discard the tough outer layer of the fennel and finely shave the bulb. Fillet the orange by removing the skin and slicing into thin slices. Trim the base of the endive and separate the leaves.

To make the dressing, in a bowl whisk together the olive oil, vinegar, mustard, cream, parsley and black pepper.

Mix salad ingredients together and drizzle over dressing. Throw in the olives, toss together and serve. Scatter with fennel fronds, if available.

Celeriac Remoulade, with Oven Roasted Prawns

This is wonderful, fresh and very simple dish relying on the essence of seasonal produce. Celeriac is a winter root vegetable, which hangs on just long enough to accompany a handful of roasted prawns doused in sea salt and ground star anise.

Serves: 2

1 large bulb of celeriac
Juice of 1 lemon
3 tbs basic mayonnaise (see recipe on page 86)
1 tbs Dijon mustard
20 medium sized green prawns (shrimp)
1 tsp ground star anise*
Sea salt and cracked black pepper
2 cups rocket/arugula
1 pink grapefruit, segmented

Peel the skin from the celeriac bulb and then slice into 3mm/⅛ inch rounds. Slice into thin julienne strips and toss in lemon juice to prevent browning. Combine the celeriac with the mayonnaise and mustard, mix well and allow to sit for 20 minutes in the refrigerator.

Peel the prawns, removing the head and outer shell but leaving the tail intact. Sprinkle the prawns with the ground star anise, salt and pepper, place onto a tray and into a fierce oven (240°C/465°F) until cooked through, approximately 3 minutes.

To serve, toss the prawns through the celeriac remoulade and scatter with the rocket leaves and grapefruit segments.

*Star anise is available from the spice section of your supermarket. Leave out if unavailable.

 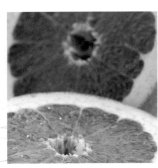

BBQ Chicken and Radicchio Salad

Serves: 6

This salad is about convenience, perfect for a picnic or a last minute dinner option. When you can easily stop off and pick up a BBQ chicken and a few fresh salad ingredients, it's put together in a matter of moments.

2 tbs olive oil

2 tsp red wine vinegar

1 tbs wholegrain mustard

Salt and freshly ground black pepper, to taste

1 whole BBQ chicken, flesh removed from bone, and broken into bite sized pieces

1 Spanish (red) onion, finely sliced

1 small head radicchio*

Garnish - Optional
2 tbs of Red Garnet (bulls blood) or opal (purple) basil

Make a dressing in a large serving bowl using the oil, vinegar and mustard and add enough seasoning to taste, only a little of each though.

Add remaining ingredients and gently toss.

*If radicchio is unavailable, red treviso, witlof or torn iceberg or romaine lettuce leaves can be used.

Roasted Beetroot and Goats Cheese Salad

A delicious starter to any meal, this compound salad has a wonderful mix of texture and flavour, not to mention it's chock full of goodness. I've used a delicious French matured goats cheese. A goats curd would be just as elegant.

Serves: 2

10 small red beetroot (beets)

Salt and freshly ground black pepper, to taste

Ciabatta loaf (waxy textured Italian style bread)

½ clove garlic

2 tbs olive oil

1 tbs red wine vinegar

150g (5oz) green beans, (blanched in boiling salted water until tender then refreshed under cold water)

40g (1½ oz) matured goats cheese

¼ bunch basil leaves

To prepare the beets for roasting, scrub under cold running water to remove any dirt. Sprinkle with a little oil and season with salt and pepper. Wrap each beetroot individually in foil and roast in a preheated, moderate to hot oven (180 to 200°C/350 to 400°F) for around 40 minutes. To test if ready, push a skewer into the larger of the beetroots (beets), there should be no resistance. Remove from oven and cool for 20 minutes. Feel free to peel the skin by pushing skin away using fingertips, however not necessary if scrubbed well.

To prepare the ciabatta, slice as fine as possible (you only need 6 pieces). Place in a medium to low oven for a few minutes to dry out until crisp.

To prepare the dressing, perfume a bowl with garlic by rubbing the cut side over the surface of the bowl, then discard clove. Add the olive oil and vinegar along with a pinch of salt and pepper.

To serve, toss beans, beets, crumbled dried ciabatta and goats cheese through dressing and assemble on a plate. Scatter with basil leaves and serve.

98

Green Olive and Potato Salad

Serves: 6

Note: To hard boil an egg. Place the room temperature egg into a pot of boiling water for 12 minutes. Remove straight away and chill under cold water before peeling.

If you can, try and get a hold of the lime green Sicilian olives, they are distinctive looking and so good.

700g (1½ lb) kipfler potatoes (scrubbed clean)
3 tbs ready made mayonnaise
Squeeze lemon juice
½ tsp paprika
Salt and freshly ground black pepper, to taste
6 hard boiled eggs, peeled and quartered
½ cup green olive cheeks
150g goats feta (shaved parmesan or pecorino is also nice)
½ bunch chives, cut into 7.5cm/3 inch lengths

Place the potatoes in a large pot, cover with cold water and bring to the boil, lower heat to a simmer and cook until tender, approximately 30 to 40 minutes. When cooked, remove from water and allow to cool, then peel and slice into thick pieces.

Mix the mayonnaise, lemon juice, paprika, salt and pepper together in a large serving bowl. Fold through remaining ingredients and potatoes. Serve.

Keeps in an airtight container in the refrigerator for up to 2 days.

Fresh Figs with Roquefort

This would have to be the sexiest way to start any meal and probably the quickest dish you would ever prepare. It does however rely upon the availability of the freshest, fattest, plumpest figs you can possibly find. When available the Black Genoa is by far the best to use, I think.

4 ripe figs
60ml (2 fl oz) verjuice*
cracked black pepper
120g (4 oz) Roquefort (blue cheese)
2 tbs extra virgin olive oil

Slice the figs in half, drizzle liberally with verjuice. Season with the cracked black pepper and scatter over the crumbled cheese and serve.

Serves: 4

Note: If Roquefort is unavailable, you can also use Gorgonzola cheese.

* Verjuice is unfermented green grape juiced. If Verjuice is unavailable, squeeze over a little fresh lime juice.

If available, also sprinkle with Red Garnet or Chervil.

102

"let food be your medicine and medicine be your food".

hippocrates

Potato Salad

Serves: 4

In Australia, it's a well known custom for someone to bring the potato salad when hosting a BBQ, here's a classic one I remember from my childhood that still serves me well, it's quick and very simple. I have given a recipe that makes enough for 4 people as a side dish. If you ever get asked to a barbecue and your job is to bring the potato salad, just multiply the recipe according to the number of people. Feel free to experiment with other ingredients; it can seriously be as simple as potatoes and mayonnaise.

400g (14 oz) kipfler or pink eye potatoes, scrubbed clean
1 cup baby green beans, steamed till tender
3 tbs of mustard cress (optional)
2 hard boiled eggs, peeled and quartered
2 tbs mayonnaise
1 tbs extra virgin olive oil
3 tbs fresh oregano leaves (dried)
Salt and freshly ground black pepper, to taste

Place the potatoes into a saucepan of cold water and bring to the boil. Cook until tender, approximately 25 to 30 minutes. Potatoes are cooked when a skewer or a small knife can be pushed into the potato with no resistance. Remove from heat and drain away the water, cool for 5 minutes.

Mix all ingredients together, with the addition of enough salt and pepper to create a balanced flavour.

Pear, Parmesan and Radicchio Salad

Perfect served alongside a piece of simply grilled fish or chicken.

1 clove garlic
Juice of half a lemon
2 tbs olive oil
Salt and freshly ground black pepper, to taste
1 small head of red treviso/radicchio
A small handful of rocket/arugula leaves
40g (1 oz) Parmesan, shaved
1 pear, preferably crisp

In a bowl large enough to hold the salad, take the clove of garlic and bruise it in the bottom of the bowl. Rub it around the bowl to leave only the juice, then discard the clove.

Squeeze in the juice of half a lemon along with the oil and seasoning. Throw in the separated and washed head of red treviso/radicchio, along with the rocket leaves and shaved Parmesan.

Thinly slice the pear, (it is not necessary to remove the core), and add to the salad. Gently toss and serve.

Zucchini Spaghetti

Serves: 2

I will try just about anything to get the kids more interested in vegetables; my son eats just about everything I put in front of him, so far so good.

2 large zucchini, approximately 240g (8$^{1}/_{2}$ oz)
1 clove garlic, finely chopped
2 tbs extra virgin olive oil
Salt and freshly ground black pepper

To prepare the zucchini, take a large knife or mandolin (a piece of kitchen equipment used for slicing) top and tail the zucchini then cut into thin strips. You may find it easier cutting the zucchini into strips if you remove a thickish slice from one side of the zucchini therefore giving you a flat surface of stability to work from. Then cut into long straws by laying slices flat on the board a few at a time.

Take the zucchini, garlic, olive oil and a little salt and pepper along with $^{1}/_{3}$ of a cup (80ml/2½ fl oz) of water and place into a medium sized saucepan, with tight-fitting lid. Bring to a boil, lower heat and cook for 2 minutes then remove from heat.

To serve drain off excess water, twist onto a plate using tongs to give a little height.

Witlof and Parmesan Salad

This is that little side salad that sits perfectly with a heavier meat based pasta.

Serves: 2

1 clove garlic
1 tbs balsamic vinegar
2 tbs extra virgin olive oil
Salt and freshly ground black pepper
1 large head of white witlof (Belgium Endive)
2 tbs finely grated Parmesan cheese

Rub a serving bowl with a piece of bruised garlic. Discard the clove once used.

Into the bowl add the vinegar, oil and a small amount of seasoning.

Throw in the separated leaves of witlof, scatter with the Parmesan cheese, toss well and serve.

If witlof is unavailable, salad greens can also be used.

"It's bizarre that the produce manager is more important to my children's health than the paediatrician".

meryl streep

Asparagus and White Peach Salad

Serves: 2

This is perfect for a weekend brunch, during summer.

1 bunch asparagus, ends trimmed

1 white peach, firm yet ripe

1 tbs hazelnut oil

1 tbs olive oil

Lime juice

Salt and freshly ground black pepper

10 fresh basil leaves

6 paper thin slices of prosciutto

¼ cup roasted hazelnuts, chopped

Blanch the asparagus in plenty of boiling salted water till tender to the tooth or al dente. (Approximately 5 minutes depending on size). Cut asparagus into 5cm (2 inch) lengths.

Split the peach in half, remove the stone and cut each half into 4 pieces.

Make a dressing with the oils, adding a little lime juice, enough to give you a slight tangy flavour, (approximately 1 teaspoon). Season with salt and pepper.

Assemble the ingredients by tossing peach and asparagus through dressing, lay on a plate interlacing the basil leaves and prosciutto and scatter with hazelnuts. Serve.

Sautéed Mushrooms with Butter and Garlic

I love it when winter comes around, after the first few frosts we get clusters of field mushrooms popping up in our back yard, straight from the ground and into the pan within seconds, barely enough time to remove the dirt.

This recipe allows for some of the more exotic varieties

Serves: 2

400g (14 oz) mixed mushrooms, sliced (a selection of oyster, Swiss browns, Enoki, Black fungus, chestnut etc)
1 tbs olive oil
1 tbs butter
2 cloves garlic, sliced
Squeeze lemon juice
¼ cup (60ml/2 fl oz) chicken stock
2 tbs chopped flat parsley

114

Cut mushrooms into good rustic chunks. Heat oil and butter in a large frying pan, add garlic and cook until golden. Add mushrooms, cooking until lightly browned. Stir in lemon juice and chicken stock and reduce moisture by half. Season, sprinkle over parsley and serve.

Vegetable Curry

Serves: 6

This sumptuous, fragrant curry may look long winded in the ingredients list, but is worth every mouthful. Not only is it low in fat, but it's packed with goodness.

This dish keeps well and tastes even better the day after cooking. For the meat lovers, you can also add 400g (14 oz) of meat, fish or chicken.

1 Spanish (red) onion, cut into small dice

1 bunch coriander, leaves picked, roots washed and finely chopped

1 knob of ginger, finely chopped

2 tbs olive oil

1 tbs fennel seeds

1 tsp crushed coriander seeds

1 tsp cumin seeds, ground

1 tsp ground turmeric

⅓ tsp ground chilli flakes, (If you like your curries hot, add a little more)

2 medium carrots, peeled and cut into 1cm cubes

1 small butternut pumpkin cut into 1 cm cubes

1 bulb of roasted garlic, (pre roasted in oven for 20 minutes at 180°C/350°F)

1 can (400ml) coconut milk (light)

420g (15 oz) can crushed tomatoes

3 tsp rice wine vinegar

1 cup (250ml/8 fl oz) of water

1 head of broccoli, cut into florets

1 bunch silverbeet, washed and shredded

Salt and freshly ground black pepper

In a heavy-based saucepan sweat the onion, coriander roots (reserve the leaves) and ginger in olive oil until translucent, about 2 to 3 minutes over a medium heat.

Add all the dry spices and stir until fragrant, approximately 2 to 3 minutes.

Lower the heat; add the carrot, pumpkin and garlic along with remaining wet ingredients. Simmer for around 20 to 25 minutes.

To prepare the greens, place into a medium sized saucepan along with ½ cup (125ml/4 fl oz) of water and bring to a boil with lid on. Simmer for a further 2 minutes then remove from heat. Leave vegetables to steam for a further 3 minutes then add to the curry.

Before serving, throw in small handful of roughly chopped coriander leaves; adjust seasoning with a little salt and pepper. Serve with steamed rice.

Pumpkin Soup with Pistou

Here's an old favourite with a new twist. The pistou takes this humble soup to a new planet, perfect in the cooler months.

Serves: 2

1 large onion, finely chopped

2 tbs olive oil

1 kg (2.2lb) pumpkin, peeled, seeded and diced

1 can (400g) cannellini beans, well drained

1 litre (1¾ pints) vegetable stock

Salt and freshly ground black pepper, to taste

In a large saucepan over moderate heat, sweat the onion in the olive oil until translucent, approximately 5 minutes.

Add the pumpkin and beans and pour over the stock. Cover with a lid and simmer for 25 minutes or until pumpkin has softened.

Remove from heat and cool slightly before pureeing in a blender. The soup should be thick and velvety but not stodgy; you can add extra stock or water, if required.

Return to the heat and season with salt and pepper. To serve, ladle into warmed bowls or mugs and drizzle with pistou and a little extra virgin olive oil.

The Pistou

Sounds like pesto and taste like pesto, is it pesto? No its Pistou! It has no pine nuts in it.

3 cloves garlic

Pinch of salt

½ bunch basil, leaves only

30g (1 oz) grated parmesan

100ml (3 ¼ fl oz) olive oil

Pepper

In a mortar and pestle, crush garlic and salt to a smooth paste. Add the basil leaves and crush to a blended paste. Add Parmesan and then the olive oil a little at a time creating a smooth emulsion. Finish with salt and pepper to taste. This sauce will keep refrigerated for a good 3 to 4 days but must be airtight.

Mashed Potato

Mashed potato goes with just about everything; my favourite mashing potato is certainly the humble, creamy Desiree.

500g (1.1 lb) large Desiree potatoes, peeled and cut into chunks
30g (1 oz) butter, roughly cubed
50ml (1½ fl oz) olive oil
½ cup (125ml/4 fl oz) warm milk
salt and ground white pepper, to taste
Pinch of nutmeg

Place potatoes in a saucepan of cold water. Bring to the boil and cook until tender, about 20 minutes

Drain and return to saucepan. Cook, shaking pan for about 20 seconds to remove excess moisture. Mash potatoes, off the heat, until smooth using a masher or preferably push through a ricer or mouli into a bowl.

Alternate beating in the butter, oil and milk until smooth and well mixed. Season with salt, white pepper and nutmeg.

121

Braised Carrots with Cumin

The cumin adds a wonderful earthiness to these sweet little baby carrots.

1 bunch baby carrots
1 tbs butter
2 tbs extra virgin olive oil
20g (¾ oz) ground cumin
100ml (3¼ fl oz) chicken stock

Trim the carrot tops and then peel or scrub.

Heat the butter and olive oil in a medium sized saucepan over a moderate heat. Add in cumin, sweating until fragrant, approximately 1 minute.

Toss in the prepared carrots along with chicken stock and cover with a tight-fitting lid or a piece of aluminium foil. Simmer the carrots until tender. Serve at once.

Tomato & Olive Crushed Potatoes

60ml (2fl oz) olive oil

400g (14 oz) waxy potatoes (kipfler, pink eye), steamed and peeled

2 tomatoes blanched, refreshed and skin removed

¼ cup green olive cheeks

Salt and freshly ground black pepper

Serves: 4

In a wide pan, warm the olive oil. Add the potatoes and work into the warmed oil with a fork, breaking and crushing the potatoes as you go. Add the tomatoes and continue to crush. You are trying to reach a coarse emulsified puree. Fold in olive cheeks and seasoning.

Garlic Crushed Potatoes

This is basically a rustic mashed potato, the waxy potatoes used here give it an amazing texture.

Serves: 4

500g (1.1 lb) waxy potatoes (kipfler, pink eye, pink fir apples, la ratte etc)

1 head of garlic

125ml (4 fl oz) olive oil

Sea salt and freshly ground black pepper

Steam the potatoes (whole and unpeeled) until cooked through, approximately 35 minutes. Cool slightly and peel.

Whilst potatoes are cooking, roast the whole head of garlic in a moderate oven 190°C (375°F) until it's soft to the touch, at least a good 25 minutes.

Once garlic has cooled a little, cut the base off and squeeze the flesh out into a heavy-based pan, throw in the peeled potatoes, crushing them between your fingers as you go. Over a moderate to low flame warm the potatoes and garlic working in the olive oil with a fork, crushing and combining with the potatoes. Season and serve.

Creamy Winter Root Vegetables

Serves: 4

This is a beautiful way to prepare some of the best of what winter has to offer. Its creamy texture is balanced with the light aniseed notes coming through from the fennel, celeriac and star anise. A great addition to a roasted chicken.

300g (10 ½ oz) fennel (trimmed weight)

200g (7 oz) waxy potatoes (desiree or kipfler)

300g (10 ½ oz) celeriac (peeled weight)

Juice of half a lemon

2 cloves of garlic, peeled and warmed in a pan with 50ml (1 ½ fl oz) olive oil for 3 minutes

80ml (2 ½ fl oz) double cream

salt and freshly ground black pepper

a pinch of ground star anise

1 tbs chopped parsley

Cut all the vegetables into even sized chunks. Steam the fennel and potatoes until tender. Boil the celeriac in salted water, with a little lemon juice to keep it from browning.

When all the vegetables are cooked, place them into a wide based pan over a gentle heat and work with a wooden spoon to dry them out.

Transfer to a food processor and make a fine puree. Work in the strained oil infusion, transfer the puree back to the pan over a gentle heat and work in the cream.

Season with salt and pepper, star anise and lemon juice. Add the parsley and keep warm until ready to serve.

Beetroot Couscous

This is one of those quick and simple side dishes that lends itself to just about anything.

Serves: 4 small servings

1½ cup (300g/10½ oz) cous cous (medium sized grain)*
3 tbs (60ml/2 fl oz) extra virgin olive oil
425g (15 oz) can sliced beetroot, drained and finely chopped
1 tomato, finely diced
½ bunch parsley, finely chopped
Salt and freshly ground black pepper

Place cous cous and olive oil into a bowl. Pour over 1½ cups (375ml/12 fl oz) of boiling water and cover to seal in heat. Leave for 10 minutes or until all moisture has been absorbed.

Drag a fork through the cous cous to break up the large lumps. When you've achieved a loose sand-like texture, fold through remaining ingredients, adding only enough salt and pepper to taste. Serve.

*Cooked rice can also be substituted if cous cous is not available.

Caramelised Witlof with Pancetta and Parmesan

Serves: 2

Witlof/Belgium endive is quite a bitter leaf when eaten raw, but that's what makes it so special.

Bitterness gives character to dishes; it breaks up the monotony of eating something sweet and untextured.

When wrapped in pancetta and roasted in butter and olive oil, it really is a dish all on its own. This is a great side dish to accompany a simple meal.

2 heads of medium sized witlof, base trimmed and halved
8 sprigs of thyme
4 slices pancetta/bacon
Salt and freshly ground black pepper
1 tbs butter
1 tbs olive oil
2 tbs shaved Parmesan
Drizzle of balsamic vinegar

Take each witlof half, top with 2 sprigs of thyme, wrap in pancetta and season. Melt butter in heavy based frying pan along with olive oil.

Place witlof in pan; cook over a moderate heat until just starting to colour then cover with baking paper. The paper will allow the witlof to steam as it caramelises.

Cook for 10 to 15 minutes until soft and golden, turning halfway. Sprinkle with Parmesan and drizzle with balsamic vinegar.

Cauliflower with White Beans and Rocket

Coming up with new ways to cook vegetables can be frustrating; the important rule is just to keep it simple. The idea though is to retain the integrity of each vegetable and this dish certainly does that.

Serves: 4

1 head cauliflower (300g)
1 clove garlic, finely chopped
3 tbs (60ml/2 fl oz) olive oil
1 can (400g) cannellini beans, drained
1 bunch rocket/arugula
Salt and freshly ground black pepper

Cut the cauliflower into small florets, discarding the stalk.

In a large frying pan with tight-fitting lid, lightly fry the garlic in 1 tbs of the olive oil until golden. Add the cauliflower along with ⅓ cup (80ml/2½ fl oz) water, the remaining olive oil and the white beans. Cover with lid and gently cook for about 8 minutes.

Remove lid and throw in torn rocket leaves along with a pinch of salt and a good grinding of fresh pepper.

Gianni's Stuffed Artichokes

Serves: 2

Gianni is a great friend of mine, who just so happens to be an amazing cook. I helped him out for a short time with his business making hand made marzipan fruit and Italian biscuits, and for lunch he would always prepare some sort of peasant style Italian dish, one of my favourites was his stuffed artichokes.

2 large globe artichokes
1 cup fresh breadcrumbs
½ cup finely grated Parmesan cheese
¼ cup chopped flat leaf parsley
2 cloves garlic, finely chopped
1 tsp lemon zest
Salt and freshly ground black pepper
Extra virgin olive oil

133

To prepare the artichokes, cut away the stalk, revealing a flat base for the artichoke to sit upon. Remove 2 to 3 layers of the outside artichoke leaves, then putting the artichoke on its side, cut away about the top ¼ of the artichoke. Turn the artichoke on to its top and lightly push into the bench to separate the leaves.

The stuffing is very easy. Just mix the breadcrumbs, Parmesan, parsley, garlic and lemon zest along with a sprinkle of salt and pepper and just enough olive oil to bind (approximately 3 to 4 tablespoons).

Pile the stuffing evenly over the top the artichoke, hold artichoke in the palm of both hands and use your thumbs to push the stuffing in between the leaves.

Place in a heavy based saucepan, big enough to hold both artichokes, pour in enough water to come up about 1 cm from the base. Cover with a lid, place over a moderate heat and simmer gently until tender, roughly 25 to 30 minutes depending on thickness.

To serve, place onto a plate along with some of the cooking juices and a big piece of ciabatta, (waxy textured bread of Italian origin).

Fennel Braised with Sicilian Green Olives

This is a great accompaniment to a piece of roasted fish and equally as good tossed through a salad of soft poached or boiled egg, rocket/arugula, toasted pine nuts and fennel seeds, extra virgin olive oil and a splash of red wine vinegar.

Serves: 2

2 fennel bulbs
12 Sicilian green olives
2 cups (500ml/16 fl oz) chicken stock, to cover
1 lemon, sliced
zest and juice of 1 orange
Salt and freshly ground black pepper

Trim tops of fennel and reserve for garnish. Place fennel into a saucepan with olives and cover with stock. Add lemon slices, orange zest and juice and season with salt and pepper. Bring to the boil and simmer until tender. Allow to cool. Top with reserved fennel tops.

pantryelements

When you've checked out the fridge and there's nothing to eat, your next option is usually the pantry. But to the untrained eye, a feast could quite easily be bypassed.

That's right, the pantry is a veritable melting pot of magnificent meals just waiting to happen.

Dry pasta, tinned tuna and mayonnaise for example may not sound like much but can certainly lend themselves to a quick, cheap and energy packed meal for a bunch of hungry surfers.

Just make sure you keep a little stock of dried pasta, rice, tinned foods and spices in your pantry. These things all have long shelf lives and are just fantastic when you need to whip up something out of practically nothing.

On the other hand, why not try making your own gnocchi? It's easy, and you probably have all the ingredients in your pantry right now!

You'll have fun with this chapter because it contains a little bit of everything. Great tasting meals with lots of international influences, but nothing overly complicated.

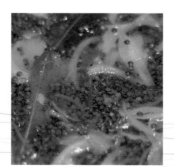

Potato Gnocchi with Meatballs

I'm not opposed to store bought potato gnocchi at all; it's just the passionate side of me that loves to make a meal like this from start to finish. I love the smell of the warm gnocchi as you roll it on a floured board.

The rich sauce with these little pillows of love is such a great marriage. Any uncooked gnocchi will freeze well, providing you store it in small batches. When it comes to defrosting, turn the frozen gnocchi into boiling salted water.

Serves: 4

The gnocchi

500g (1lb) Desiree potatoes, not peeled

170g (6 oz) plain flour

2 tbs olive oil

1½ tsp salt

¼ tsp nutmeg

freshly ground black pepper

¼ cup (20g/¾ oz) grated Parmesan

For the meatballs

500g (1lb) lean mince

1 small onion, finely chopped

1 egg

3 tbs Worcestershire sauce

1 tbs dried rosemary

Salt and freshly ground black pepper

Plain flour, for dusting

The sauce

¼ cup (60ml/2 fl oz) olive oil

1 clove garlic, sliced

5 anchovy fillets (optional)

1 small chilli, finely chopped

400g (14 oz) can peeled tomatoes

¼ cup chopped parsley

Extra parmesan

141

Note: A mouli or ricer is relatively inexpensive, and is something you would find at a kitchen equipment store. Just mashing the potatoes will give you rough gnocchi that is hard to work with.

Gnocchi

Place potatoes in a steamer over simmering water. Cover and cook for 20 minutes or until tender. Cool slightly, peel and pass through a mouli or a ricer*.

Sieve the flour over the potatoes along with olive oil, seasonings and Parmesan. You may need to use more or less flour depending on how wet the potatoes are. Gently knead dough being careful not to overwork, as it makes the gnocchi tough and doughy.

Divide dough into 6 pieces. Roll each piece out until 2cm (¾ inch) thick and about 40cm (15 inch) long. Cut into 1cm (½ inch) 'pillows'. Set aside.

Bring a large pot of salted water to the boil. Just before serving cook gnocchi in batches until they float to the surface. Remove with a slotted spoon. Serve immediately.

Meatballs

For the meatballs, mix all ingredients except flour together until well combined. This is quite a moist mixture; don't feel the need to add flour. Roll into balls the size of a cherries and dust in flour.

In a deep pan, heat olive oil along with sliced garlic, anchovies and chilli. Add meat balls and cook until evenly browned. Pour over the can of tomatoes, cover, lower temperature and simmer for 5 minutes, or until cooked through. Season to taste and finish with parsley.

To serve, nap** the gnocchi with the meatballs. Top with more Parmesan if desired.

**Nap. To gently spoon the sauce over the gnocchi.

Chilled Buckwheat Noodles with Salmon and Toasted Nori

Chilled noodles may not sound like the most appetising of dishes, but trust me they are well worth the effort. The noodles can be cooked well in advance, making sure they are refreshed after cooking in plenty of cold running water and drained well to stop sticking. This dish tastes as good as it looks.

Serves: 2

180g (6¾ oz) buckwheat noodles

1 tbs olive oil

220g (7¾ oz) salmon, skin and bones removed

1 sheet of Nori*

I tsp sesame oil

1 small Lebanese cucumber

2 tbs pickled ginger

1 tbs black sesame seeds (toasted white seeds would also be fine)

2 tbs light soy sauce

6 sprigs fresh coriander

1 fresh lime

salt for water

Plunge the buckwheat noodles into a pot of salted boiling** water and cook till soft, leaving a light nutty texture.

Heat the olive oil in a small but heavy-based saucepan till hot or when a blue haze appears. Lay the piece of salmon in the pan and cook for 3 to 4 minutes then turn and cook to desired doneness. I prefer the salmon cooked to medium rare so a cooking time of around 8 minutes all up; this certainly varies due to the thickness of the salmon. Once cooked set aside and allow to rest for 5 minutes.

Prepare the Nori by placing on a baking tray drizzled with the sesame oil and toast in a hot oven (200°C/400°F) for 5 to 6 minutes or till crisp. Cool slightly then crumble into pieces.

Using a vegetable peeler, peel ribbons from the cucumber, discarding the centre seeded section.

To assemble, break the salmon into smaller pieces, toss through the noodles with cucumber, pickled ginger, sesame seeds, toasted Nori pieces, sesame oil and soy sauce.

Serve topped with coriander sprigs and a wedge of lime.

* Nori are sheets of seaweed found in the Asian section of your supermarket.

**Water should taste like the sea without being overly salty.

Doms No Frills Pasta

Serves: 3 hungry surfers for under A$5.00

Note: For a little added flavour don't hesitate to give the pasta a wave with the pepper grinder, and a scattering of fresh parsley or basil.

I was about 19 years of age, completing my Commercial Cookery trade certificate, working no less than 60 hours a week in a high profile restaurant and surfing every other waking hour. I was renting with two guys Chris and Dom, we all worked and surfed together.

Dom had a knack for whipping up something out of nothing and to this day he is still an inspiration. For about $5.00 he could feed three very hungry lads and leave them very satisfied. I don't cook this pasta so much anymore but for those on a budget, this dish is tailored to you.

500g (1lb) generic brand linguine or spaghetti
400g (14 oz) can generic brand tuna, drained
1½ cups (450g/1lb) generic brand whole egg mayonnaise

Cook the pasta following the packet instructions, in plenty of boiling salted water for approximately 10 to 12 minutes depending on quality of pasta. It should be ever so slightly nutty.

When cooked, drain pasta well, add the drained tuna and mayonnaise, mix well and serve.

145

"all you see, i owe to spaghetti." sophia loren.

Lasagne with Crab and Tomato

I love lasagne, no question about it. My biggest frustration when eating out is someone else's interpretation of it. Too many times it's this big mass of stodge, lacking in flavour… and layers, give me layers!

I believe that a good lasagne should have at least 7 very thin layers of pasta, a well-seasoned velvety sauce and a portion size which is sufficient but doesn't leave you bloated.

Here's my take on an Italian classic with the inclusion of sweet crab meat (one of the seven wonders of the sea). Any fresh crab or lobster will do here. I've used rocket, a wonderful spinach-like leaf with a peppery quality that leaves a tangy note on the tongue. Spinach or sorrel could be substituted here.

Serves: 2

4 x 30cm (12 inch) fresh pasta sheets, or dried pasta sheets

1 tbs butter

1 tbs olive oil

2 tbs flour

400ml (12¾ fl oz) milk

2 tbs tomato paste

150g (5⅓ oz) crab meat, in the shell about

500g (1 lb)

1 large ripe tomato, finely chopped

1 cup rocket (arugula), stems removed

¼ cup (15g/ ½ oz) fresh or dried breadcrumbs*

2 tbs extra virgin olive oil

If dried pasta sheets are being used, cook following the instructions on packet. If you have fresh pasta, lightly blanch in boiling, salted water for a few seconds and then refresh in iced water to stop overcooking. Drain and pat dry, set aside.

Prepare the sauce by melting the butter and olive oil in a saucepan over a moderate heat. Mix in the flour and cook for a few minutes. Gradually add the milk a little at a time, mixing well after each addition. Keep stirring over a low to moderate heat. When all milk has been added whisk in the tomato paste. The sauce will need to cook for at least 10 minutes to cook away the starchy quality of the flour.

Line the base of a small ovenproof dish with a thin layer of the sauce, then top with a sheet of pasta, a layer of sauce, then crab, alternate layers of sauce, pasta and crab with every third layer having the addition of a scattering of fresh tomato and rocket leaves. The seventh layer is to be topped with sauce only, then the breadcrumbs and a splash of extra virgin olive oil.

Place into a preheated oven of 200°C (400°F) for 15 to 20 minutes till heated through and the breadcrumbs are crisp and golden. Allow 5 minutes to rest before serving. Serve accompanied with a little green salad.

* To make fresh breadcrumbs, place day old bread into a blender or food processor and pulse for a few seconds.

Linguini with Seared Tuna and Tapenade

Serves: 2

Note: Parmesan cheese is not necessary (to dress this dish) given the complexity of the olive paste with the addition of extra capers.

This is a recipe I remember vividly as it tantalised a large number of palates when I was an apprentice at Mark Armstrong's, *Armstrong's Restaurant* in Manly, Sydney, Australia.

Relatively simple, if fresh tuna is not available substitute canned. If you have trouble finding a prepared tapenade, I have given a recipe to make your own. Your tastebuds will thank you for your efforts.

150g (5 ⅓ oz) linguini
3 tbs olive oil
1 small chilli, seeds removed and finely chopped
240g (8 ½ oz) fresh tuna, cut into 2cm (¾ inch) cubes
3 tbs tapenade (see page 70)
1 roasted red capsicum (bell pepper), blackened skin and seeds removed
Small handful of rocket (arugala) leaves
3 tbs torn flat parsley leaves
½ small bunch picked basil leaves
2 tbs extra virgin olive oil
salt for water

Bring a large saucepan of salted water to the boil. Cook pasta according to instructions on the packet. Drain and set aside.

Heat 1 tbs (20ml/ ½ fl oz) of the oil in a large, thick based frying pan, add chilli and tuna, lightly seasoned with salt and pepper. Cook on a medium heat for about 30 seconds. Stir in tapenade, capsicum, rocket (arugala) and parsley. Add cooked pasta and toss to coat.

To serve, using a pair of tongs twist the pasta into a tornado shape and serve in a warm bowl. Top with a little torn basil and extra virgin olive oil.

Lumache with Sicilian Chickpea Stew

This is a great vegetarian dish. Served warm or cold, both options are delicious.   Serves: 4

200g lumache or other shell shaped pasta

3 tbs olive oil

1 Spanish (red) onion, diced

1 large carrot, peeled and diced

1 stalk celery, peeled, leaves removed and diced

1 tsp fennel seeds

½ tsp paprika

Juice and zest of one orange

½ cup (125ml/4 fl oz) dry white wine/verjuice*

400g (14 oz) can chickpeas, drained

4 Roma tomatoes, peeled, seeded and roughly chopped

6 large leaves of silverbeet, stalk removed and roughly shredded

3 tbs chopped parsley

Salt and freshly ground black pepper, to taste

Cook pasta following packet instructions. When cooked rinse under plenty of cold water to wash away excess starch and to stop over cooking, set aside.

Heat olive oil in a large pan over a medium heat, add the onion, carrot, celery and fennel seeds. Cook slowly for about 15minutes or until carrots are tender. Add paprika, orange zest and juice, white wine and cook until liquid is almost reduced.

Add chickpeas, tomatoes, silverbeet and parsley. Finish with a good pinch of salt and pepper. Allow to sit and steep for 20 minutes before serving. Fold through cooked pasta and serve.

*Verjuice is unfermented green grape juice.

Orecchiette with Minted Lentils and Gremolata

Serves: 4

Orecchiette is a small 'ear' shaped pasta that works perfectly with this dish. The pasta doubles as a little cup and picks up the sweet softened lentils along with the peppery rocket to give you an array of flavour and texture.

150g (5 ⅓ oz) orecchiette

200g (7 oz) braised lentils, recipe follows or a can of pre-cooked lentils

2 tbs mint leaves

2 tbs extra virgin olive oil

salt and freshly ground black pepper

zest of 1 orange, finely chopped

1 clove garlic, finely chopped

¼ cup chopped flat leaf parsley

2 cups baby rocket (arugula)

Bring a large saucepan of salted water to the boil. Drop orecchiette into the water and cook according to the packet instructions. Drain and set aside.

Warm the pre-cooked lentils over a moderate heat, stir through torn mint, extra virgin olive oil and season with salt and pepper.

To make the Gremolata mix the orange zest, garlic and parsley together.

To serve toss the drained pasta, lentils and rocket together. Spoon into serving bowls and scatter with the gremolata

Minted Lentils

Once cooked, the lentils will keep for a good 4 to 5 days as long as they are well chilled. A delicious accompaniment to a piece of grilled fish, or even thinned out and served with a soft boiled egg and crusty bread as a soup.

1 large onion, finely sliced

3 cloves garlic, finely sliced

1 fresh bay leaf

½ cup (125ml/4 fl oz) extra virgin olive oil

500g (1lb) green lentils, well rinsed

50ml (1½ fl oz) balsamic vinegar

¼ bunch fresh mint

Salt and freshly ground black pepper

In a heavy based pan, lightly sweat the onion, garlic and bay leaf in the olive oil till translucent. Add the rinsed lentils and cover with cold water. Turn heat to medium and continue to cook till soft, approximately 40 minutes. You may need to top up the water to keep lentils submerged. When lentils are soft, add the balsamic, the mint, including stalks, season to taste and allow to cool.

When cool remove bay leaf and mint.

Paella

A Spanish feast like this deserves to be shared among good friends with an ice cold beer. The freshest of seafood is essential.

Serves: 6

2 tbs olive oil

250g (8¾ oz) chicken thigh fillets, cut into 3cm (1 inch) pieces

1 chorizo sausage, skinned and sliced

1 red capsicums (bell pepper), sliced

1 Spanish (red) onion, finely chopped

2 cloves garlic, crushed

1 tsp smoked Spanish paprika

2½ cups (500g/1lb) short grain or Spanish rice

1 cup (250ml/8 fl oz) white wine

425g (15 oz) can crushed tomatoes

4 cups (1 litre/1¾ pints) chicken stock

Generous pinch saffron, dissolved in ½ cup (125ml/4 fl oz) warm water

2 tbs chopped rosemary

18 medium sized green prawns (shrimp), peeled

3 medium sized squid, cleaned, scored and cut into smaller pieces*

1 cup (120g/4 oz) peas

¼ cup chopped parsley

Heat olive oil in a large shallow pan (preferably a paella pan). Add chicken and cook until browned. Remove.

Add sausage, capsicums and onion. Cook, stirring, until chorizo is browned and onions are soft. Stir in garlic and paprika. Cook for 30 seconds.

Add rice and stir to coat with capsicum mixture. Pour in wine and cook until nearly absorbed. Add tomatoes, stock, saffron and rosemary. Cook on low heat for 15 minutes. Return chicken to the pan along with the prawns and squid. Cook a further 5 minutes. Stir through peas and cook a further 3 minutes. Stir through parsley and serve immediately.

*For information on how to clean a squid, please see my DVD.

Pat's Pasta Sauce

Serves: 4

Note: I will generally make a double quantity of this recipe as it freezes well. Perfect in toasted sandwiches, savoury pastries, cannelloni etc etc or when unexpected guests turn up for dinner.

Here's a recipe from my good mate Pat Feige in the Royal Australian Navy.

This is one of those easy and quick meals after football training – just defrost the sauce, cook the pasta and within 15 minutes you're eating.

1 onion, finely chopped

2 cloves garlic

2 tbs olive oil

500g (1lb) lean mince

½ cup (125ml/4 fl oz) dry red wine

2 tbs tomato paste

400g (14 oz) can tomato soup

400g (14 oz) can crushed tomatoes

1 tsp mixed dried herbs

157

In a medium sized pan over a gentle heat, sweat the onion and garlic in olive oil until translucent. Increase the heat, add mince and cook stirring occasionally to break up any clumps until well browned.

Once browned, drain away any excess fat. Pour in the red wine and cook until almost all of the liquid has evaporated. Mix in the tomato paste, tomato soup, crushed tomatoes and dried herbs. Lower the temperature and very slowly braise the meat sauce for 1½ to 2 hours.

Serve spooned over your favourite pasta and topped with parmesan cheese.

"Since eve ate the apple, much depends on dinner".
lord byron

Pea and Ricotta Ravioli

I do enjoy making pasta, I find it therapeutic, but if I'm a little pressed for time, I never think twice about cracking open a packet of wonton wrappers. They are super convenient and stocked in the cold section of the supermarket. I'll generally pick mine up in Chinatown, along with a variety of other weird and unexpected wonderfuls.

Serves: 4

100g (3 ½ oz) frozen peas, defrosted
200g (7 oz) fresh ricotta
30g (1 oz) Parmesan cheese, finely grated
1 egg
salt and freshly ground black pepper
pinch of nutmeg
24 wonton wrappers/skins
50mls (1½ fl oz) milk

1 tbs butter
2 tbs olive oil
1 lemon, juiced
3 tbs chopped curly parsley
Olive oil
Extra Parmesan cheese for serving

With the back of a fork, lightly crush the peas with the ricotta, Parmesan and egg. Try not to turn the peas into a puree as you want to retain a little texture. Season with salt, pepper and nutmeg.

To make the ravioli, lay half of the wonton wrappers on a clean surface. Using a small spoon drop a small spoonful of ricotta mix onto the centre of each. With a pastry brush, lightly brush the edges of the wrappers with milk and then lay a second wrapper over the top of each. Press edges together, firmly, being careful not to squash the ricotta filling out.

Melt butter and olive oil in a small saucepan over a gentle heat until it turns nut-brown in colour. Immediately adding a good squeeze of lemon juice, chopped parsley, a pinch of salt and a generous grinding of fresh black pepper.

Cook the ravioli, a few at a time, in a pot of lightly salted boiling water. When the ravioli float to the surface, about 20 seconds, lift out of the water with a slotted spoon and place into lemon and butter sauce. Gently toss to coat and serve topped with parmesan.

Bucatini with Dried Chilli and Parmesan

Serves: 2

Here's a great dish for when you come home in the wee small hours of the morning after a big night out. If I have a suspicion I am going to have a late night, I will place a pot of water on the stove ready to turn on to cook the pasta, set my chopping board up with all the ingredients prepared and laid out ready to go, so as soon as I walk in the door, 15 minutes to the second later I will be eating.

150g (5½ oz) bucatini (long thin tubular pasta)
4 tbs (80ml/2½ fl oz) olive oil
2 cloves of garlic, roughly chopped
½ tsp dried chilli
7 anchovy fillets (optional)
4 tbs roughly chopped flat leaf parsley
3 tbs finely grated good quality Parmesan (Reggiano if possible)
Freshly cracked black pepper

161

Cook pasta according to packet instructions, approximately 12 minutes in plenty of boiling salted water.

Meanwhile, heat a medium-sized pan over moderate heat with olive oil, garlic, chilli and anchovies. Cook until garlic turns golden and the anchovies start to break up.

Be aware that the anchovies can have a tendency to spatter a little. Remove from heat, throw in parsley followed by pasta and parmesan and give a quick toss then serve, with a good grinding of pepper.

Birthdays were a real treat growing up on our farm and it was dinner time that made the occasion really special. Our whole family used to look forward to it.

I'll never forget the big old axe, which we normally used for splitting fire wood for the stove. It would get a good swift sharpen over the stone before an unlucky candidate was chosen from the chook pen as our guest for dinner.

After plucking, preparing and roasting, we were seated at the family table with a grin from ear to ear that indicated we wanted more... even before we'd been served.

Today, of course, we buy our chicken and game birds completely pre pared, leaving us just to follow a good recipe to create a succulent result. In this chapter, you'll find some great methods and neat techniques I use to preserve the integrity of flavour, texture and moisture when cooking our fine feathered friends.

poultryelements

Salt Crust Chicken with Creamy Polenta & Beurre Noisette

Serves: 4

Salt crust cookery is an ancient technique, which seems to have its origins in Chinese cookery where poultry was packed in pure salt and baked. The method I have given is commonly used in France and uses a flour and salt dough shell to preserve the moisture and texture while intensifying the flavour.

This method of cookery also lends itself to various game, fish and certain cuts of beef.

The Salt Crust

1kg (2lb) butchers salt*

1kg (2lb) plain flour

670ml (1¼ pints) cold water

Knead the above ingredients together to form a smooth dough and rest for ½ hour.

The Stuffing

2 bunches English spinach, stems removed and leaves chopped

1 bunch sorrel or rocket (arugula), stems removed and leaves chopped

1 clove garlic, finely chopped

Cracked black pepper

1 x No.14 (1.4kg / 3lb) free range or organic chicken

The Polenta

2½ cups (625ml/1 pint) chicken stock

100g (3½ oz) white polenta (or yellow polenta if white is not available)

40g (1½ oz) butter

30g (1 oz) grated Parmesan

Pre-heat oven to 220°C/430°F.

In a saucepan wilt the spinach, sorrel and garlic until collapsed. Season with black pepper and refrigerate to cool.

Remove the chicken from packaging and drain well. If the neck is still intact, remove it using a sharp knife, being careful not to remove too much skin from around the breast. Slide your fingers, between the skin and the breast meat to form a pocket. Stuff the cooled spinach mixture into the pocket. Tie the chicken with string to secure the legs.

*Butchers Salt is a high quality washed salt with a medium crystal size used mainly for food processing.

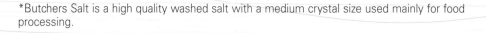

Line a baking tray with a sheet of grease proof paper. Roll the salt crust dough out until 5mm (¼ inch) thick and large enough to encase the whole chicken. Wrap the chicken in the dough, being conscious not to leave any holes. Trim away any excess. Place onto prepared baking tray.

Roast chicken for 50 minutes. The best way to test if it's done is to pierce the salt-crust with a small sharp knife near the thigh. Remove knife and feel the blade with your fingertips, it should be quite warm. Remove from oven and allow to rest for a good half an hour before cracking open the crust.

The Polenta

Meanwhile, bring the stock to the boil in a saucepan. Slowly add the polenta, whisking as you go. Reduce the heat to low and stir for 15 to 20 minutes, or until the polenta starts to pull away from the side of the pan. If too thick, thin down with a little extra water.

Stir in the butter and Parmesan along with a good grinding of fresh pepper; be aware when adding salt because the Parmesan is already salty. Cover and set aside.

To serve the chicken, remove breast meat by running a knife down the centre of the breast then leaver the meat away from the breastbone. Slice each breast in two. To remove the legs, pull the thigh away from the carcass, and cut at the joint. Cut the thigh from the drumstick.

Beurre Noisette (Nut Brown Butter)

Don't start preparing this until the polenta is cooked and the chicken is portioned.

Melt the butter in a small fry pan allowing it to gently reach a bubbly stage after which it should foam. The butter will start to take on colour once the foam subsides. At this point throw in the chopped parsley, a squeeze of lemon juice and season.

To serve, lay a piece of the breast and thigh on a little bed of the creamy polenta and nap with the beurre noisette.

Stir-fried Chicken with Baby Corn & Basil

I love cooking with a wok, its quick and easy one pot cooking at its best, a bachelor's best friend!

Serve and eat this one straight away.

2 tbs olive oil

250g (8 oz) chicken thigh fillets, sliced

3 long red chillies, seeds removed and finely sliced

1 clove garlic, finely sliced

2cm (1 inch) knob of ginger, finely sliced

2 tbs oyster sauce

1 tbs fish sauce

1 tbs brown sugar

¼ cup chicken stock (or water)

200g (7 oz) baby corn

½ cup basil leaves (optional)

1 lime

169

Heat oil in a wok until just smoking.

Add chicken and stir-fry until golden. Pour off any excess oil then toss in chilli, garlic and ginger. Stir-fry for 30 seconds, add the stock, oyster and fish sauces, sugar and baby corn. Cook for a further 30 seconds, finishing with the fresh basil and a squeeze of lime.

Spoon onto a serving plate accompanied with a bowl of steamed rice.

Chicken Breast Stuffed with Tarragon Quenelle on Tomato & Olive Crushed Potatoes

I was invited to New Zealand a few years ago to create a winter menu for a restaurant in Auckland called "Amadeus on the Boulevard". It took lots of hard work to get the menu up and running and was certainly a learning curve. This particular dish was a huge success, not a quick recipe by any means. I suggest reading the method a couple of times before attempting, seriously worth the effort though. See page 122 for the crushed potatoes recipe.

Serves: 6

As an option, you can serve this dish with braised carrots and cumin, see page 121.

60g (2oz) crustless white bread

120ml (3¾ fl oz) single cream

220g (7¾ oz) chicken breast meat, skin and sinew removed and chopped

1 egg

¼ tsp salt

200ml (6½ fl oz) cream, extra

White pepper

A few leaves of fresh tarragon, chopped

Nutmeg

6 chicken breasts Frenched, skin on and the wing bone trimmed

hot chicken stock, for poaching

Preheat oven to 160°C (320°F). Soak bread in cream for 5 minutes until soft. Puree chicken meat in a blender until smooth. For best results, keep all ingredients well chilled.

In a large bowl over an ice-bath (see Note), beat egg, salt, creamed bread and pureed chicken until a firm mix has formed. In a fine stream and while beating, pour in the extra cream to form a light creamy mousse. Season with pepper, tarragon and nutmeg. Place the mousse mixture into a piping bag.

To prepare the chicken breasts, push your index finger between the flesh and skin of the wing end of the breast to make a pocket. (Be careful not to pierce the thin connective membrane). Pipe mousse under the skin of each breast, they should be relatively plump and firm.

Place chicken breasts into a large saucepan or a small, deep baking tray and pour over boiling chicken stock to cover then cover with a layer of foil. Place into oven and cook for about 20 to 25 minutes until chicken breasts are firm to touch. Cool in poaching liquor for a good 15 minutes.

When breasts have been allowed to cool slightly, remove from stock and cover to keep warm. Heat stock until reduced by half and serve as a sauce.

Note: The ice bath is a bowl filled with half ice and half water with a slightly smaller bowl set over the ice. This allows the chicken mousse to stay cold whilst mixing, allowing for a better emulsification.

Note: For convenience sake, this dish can be done a day in advance. The chicken will just need to be reheated thoroughly.

Chicken Breast Stuffed with Fontina and Rosemary

Serves: 2

I love this dish, not just because it is simple but also for the wonderful flavour of the cheese with dried rosemary. It's so delicious!

Depending on your tastes it can be served with a wide variety of vegetables. I like to keep it simple with roasted potatoes and asparagus or mushrooms. Here I have served it with caramelised witlof, wrapped in pancetta and also green beans. See page 129, Garden Elements.

2 chicken breasts, skin and wing bone intact
60g (2 oz) Fontina cheese
1 tbs finely chopped fresh rosemary
salt and freshly ground black pepper, to taste
2 tbs olive oil

Preheat oven to 180°C (350°F).

Holding the chicken breast by the wing, push index finger in between the flesh and the skin to separate and form a pocket.

Cut the cheese into 2 thin pieces, roll in the fresh rosemary and push under the skin of the chicken.

Heat olive oil in a frypan. Season the chicken with salt and pepper. When the pan is hot throw in the chicken, flesh side down and brown for 2 minutes. Turn and place into the oven for 8 minutes which should be ample time for the chicken to cook through. Remove from oven, wrap in foil and rest for 5 minutes before serving.

Roasted Chicken with Bay Leaf & Lemon

One of my favourite herbs would definitely be fresh bay leaf. It lends itself to a wide variety of dishes both sweet and savoury. With the addition of a punctured lemon and used to stuff a chicken, it makes for a wonderful mid-week roast.

No.15 (1.5kg/3⅓ lb) chicken
1 lemon
3 bay leaves
Olive oil
Salt and freshly ground black pepper

Serves: 4

Note: Time will differ depending on heat of your oven, remembering that no two ovens are the same. The best way to check for doneness is to slip a knife in between the thigh and rib cage to make sure any moisture running out, runs clear.

Preheat oven to 200°C (400°F). Remove chicken from packaging and pat dry with a paper towel to remove any excess moisture. Remove any extras that may be inside the cavity, eg giblets or neck.

174

Starting at the neck and using your fingers, create a pocket by gently sliding your fingers between the skin and the breast meat. When a pocket has been formed, gently push 2 of the bay leaves in to sit flat against the breast meat.

Soften the lemon by rolling it under your hand on a firm surface. This will allow the lemon to release moisture and flavour whilst cooking. Make three long cuts in the lemon, still leaving it whole and place into the chicken cavity along with the remaining bay leaf.

Take a length of butcher's string (used for roasting) about 60cm (2 feet) long and tie around the knuckle of the drumsticks, leaving an even length on either side of the bird. Pull both ends up alongside the breast enhancing the contour between thigh and breast, and tying firmly around the neck end. The idea is to plump the breast, to give a much fuller looking bird.

Douse with olive oil, season with salt and pepper and place, breast side down into a heated skillet until golden. Turn and roast in oven for approximately 40 to 45 minutes or until cooked through. Remove and rest for 10 minutes before serving.

Li'l Snizzels

Serves: 2

Note: Never over crowd the pan as this can sometimes result in the snizzles stewing and going tough. Remember you only need enough heat to heat the pan, too much heat is not only a waste of energy but will also burn the bread crumb coating.

I love li'l snizzles. Basically a chicken schnitzel, maybe a little smaller and so named to entice the young ones. The sort of dish they can even pitch in and give a hand with and they taste good too! I also love these on a sandwich with shredded lettuce and mayonnaise.

2 skinless chicken breast fillets
½ cup (80g/ 2¾ oz) wholemeal plain flour
2 eggs, lightly beaten
1 cup (100g/ 3 ½ oz) breadcrumbs (packaged or fresh)
½ cup (40g/ 1½ oz) grated Parmesan cheese
Salt and freshly ground black pepper, to taste
60ml (2 fl oz) olive oil

Split each breast in half. I find the easiest way is to place your hand firmly on top of each breast and using a sharp knife slice them into two thin pieces. Place the chicken between two sheets of plastic and beat lightly to make even thinner.

Organise yourself with the flour on a plate, beaten eggs in a good sized bowl and the breadcrumbs, mixed with parmesan and seasoned with a little salt and pepper, in a tray.

Run each piece of chicken through the flour, dusting off excess. Drench in egg, allowing excess to run off and then coat with breadcrumbs.

Heat the oil in a heavy based pan. Lower in a couple of snizzles at a time, cooking until golden and then turn. When golden on both sides drain on absorbent paper before serving. Serve with salad and a piece of lemon.

"There is no love sincerer than the love of food".
george bernard shaw, irish playwright (1856-1950)

Confit of Squab with Braised Green Lentils, Roasted Beetroot & Sauce Poivrade

I hope you don't mind but I have indulged myself by putting in a recipe that demonstrates my love and respect of French cuisine. I have a great deal of respect for French technique and the labour and love that goes into making every meal. This is a method of preparing squab/pigeon that I came up with during my time at Bistro Moncur.

Serves: 4

The Squab

4 squab/pigeon (450 to 500g/1lb) each

3 cloves garlic

1 cup coarse butchers salt*

7 sprigs thyme

1.5 litres (2.5 pints) olive oil, for poaching

Remove the legs from the birds by separating the thigh from the carcass and set aside. Using a pair of kitchen shears or a sharp knife cut along the rib cage to remove the breast plate, leaving the breast and bone joined together.

On a clean bench, crush the whole cloves of garlic, to release the aroma. Scatter ¾ of the salt over the bench then lay down the prepared legs and breast, skin side up. Scatter with bruised thyme and remaining salt. Allow to cure for 2 hours then quickly rinse off salt and pat dry with paper towel.

Heat the olive oil to 80 to 90°C (175 to 195°F) and drop in the legs and breast. Poach until firm, making sure the oil remains at a constant heat for approximately 15 to 20 minutes. Remove from oil and cool.

When cool, remove the breast meat from the bone by running your knife along the centre of the breast plate and filleting the flesh from the bone. Set aside ready to pan roast.

To serve, pan roast breast and legs skin side down in a little olive oil until golden. Turn and roast in oven for about 4 minutes at 180°C (350°F). Have other components ready to go. Onto a serving plate ladle a small scoop of the lentils, add a few beetroots. Take squab from oven and set over the lentils, nap over about 30ml (1 fl oz) of sauce poivrade and serve.

Roasted Beetroot

I have used a mixture of gold and red beets however red are far more readily available. Scrub 12 medium sized beetroot, sprinkle with a little olive oil and season with salt and pepper. Wrap each beetroot individually in foil and roast in a preheated oven (200 to 220°C/400 to 440°F) for around 40 minutes. Test if ready by pushing in a skewer, there should be no resistance. You can peel if desired, however not necessary if scrubbed well enough.

*Butchers Salt is a high quality washed salt with a medium crystal size used mainly for food processing.

***Note:** Once you have added the butter you won't be able to
re-boil the sauce as it will split.
So be aware of the timing of your dish.

The Lentils

250g (8oz) green lentils

1 medium onion

2 cloves garlic, bruised

80ml (2 ½ fl oz) extra virgin olive oil

1 bay leaf, torn

Salt and freshly ground black pepper

Wash and pick over the lentils. In a heavy based saucepan, sweat the onion and garlic in olive oil until translucent. Add lentils, cover with cold water and add bay leaf.

Bring to a boil then simmer for approximately 20 minutes until tender but not over cooked. They should still remain a little nutty in texture, add a little salt and pepper to taste.

Sauce Poivrade*

2 tbs oil

Trimmings from squab, roughly chopped

1 small carrot, peeled and roughly chopped

½ an onion, sliced

70ml (2 ¼ fl oz) red wine vinegar

50ml (1 ½ fl oz) port

50ml (1 ½ fl oz) Madeira

10 peppercorns, crushed

3 sprigs thyme

1 bay leaf

400ml (13 fl oz) game or chicken stock

30 to 40g (1oz) butter

Heat oil in a heavy based pan, add squab trimmings and cook until brown. Add carrot and onion and sweat for a few minutes.

Add vinegar, port and Madeira along with the peppercorns and herbs. Cook until reduced by two thirds then add stock and reduce again by half. Remove from the heat.

Strain sauce through a sieve into a small saucepan. Swirl in butter, a little at a time to give a glossy sheen. Season with salt and pepper. It should be both peppery and sharp to taste.

Braised Organic Chicken with Fresh Borlotti Beans & Parmesan

I love everything about winter but especially the produce. The plethora of beans, root vegetables, hearty sumptuous dishes and obviously less people out in the surf.

This dish is definitely worth every minute of the 60 it takes to make. Not only is this simple to make but it's just as comforting as a cuddle from mum.

If fresh borlotti beans are not available, canned may be used, but not added until the chicken has simmered for a good 30 to 40 minutes.

2 chicken marylands (the chicken leg & thigh)
Salt and freshly ground black pepper, to taste
2 tbs olive oil
1 onion, finely chopped
1 clove garlic
1 fresh bay leaf
2 small carrots, cut into 1cm cubes
1½ cups shelled borlotti beans
1 cup fresh rocket/ arugula
¼ cup shaved Parmesan
2 tbs extra virgin olive oil

Season the chicken pieces with salt and pepper and place into a pan doused with olive oil. Cook until both sides are golden, remove from pan and drain off excess fat.

To the pan add the onion, garlic, bay leaf, carrot and borlotti beans. Add chicken and enough water to barely cover. Bring to the boil, lower heat to a mere simmer and continue to cook until beans are soft, approximately 30 to 40 minutes. Turn off and allow to cool for 20 minutes, this allows chicken to almost fall of the bone.

Remove chicken from pan, flake the meat off the bone, return to the beans. Bring back to a boil, adjust seasoning and add fresh rocket. Top with Parmesan and a splash of extra virgin olive oil.

Five Spice Quail with Stir-Fried Cabbage

Serves: 4 small portions

Quail may not be the most accessible of ingredients to find, but when available and served in this manner, it's a real treat. Chicken could also be used in this recipe (8 chicken wings).

1½ tsp five spice powder

4 large quail (150g/5 oz) split in half

60ml (2 fl oz) fish sauce

60ml (2 fl oz) lime juice

1 tbs olive oil

1 tbs light soy sauce

1 tsp palm sugar (or brown sugar)

2 cloves garlic, finely chopped

1 birds eye chilli, seeds removed and chopped

½ white Chinese cabbage/Wombok

60ml (2 fl oz) olive oil

2 cm (1 inch) piece of fresh ginger, cut into fine strips

2 chillies, seeds removed and finely sliced lengthways

2 tbs Chinese dried prawns (soaked in boiling water for 5 minutes) – optional

Salt, to taste

30ml (1 fl oz) light soy sauce

2 shallots, finely sliced on the diagonal

½ bunch fresh coriander/cilantro

Sprinkle five-spice over quail and set aside. Combine fish sauce, lime juice, olive oil, soy sauce, sugar, garlic and chilli. Pour ⅓ of the mixture over the quail. Reserve the remaining mixture to serve at room temperature as a sauce. Turn the quails in the marinade, then cover and refrigerate for 1 hour.

Preheat oven to 200°C (400°F). Remove quail from marinade. Heat an ovenproof frying pan over a medium to high heat and add quail, breast side down. When golden turn and transfer to oven for about 6 minutes or until cooked through, but still moist.

To prepare the cabbage, clean and remove a few of the outer blemished leaves. Split the cabbage in half and finely shred.

Heat oil in a wok or a wide saucepan, when oil is warm add ginger, chilli and the drained prawns. Stir-fry over medium heat for a couple of minutes. Add cabbage, sprinkle with salt and continue to fry for a few minutes more until the cabbage has softened. Add soy sauce and finish with the shallots.

Serve a whole quail on top of the stir-fried cabbage and garnish with fresh coriander.

Roasted Guinea Fowl with Bread Sauce & Calvados

Here's an adventurous dish that is so good it should be banned. The guinea fowl could certainly be replaced with another white fleshed game bird if not available; pheasant, partridge, etc are certainly appropriate. Cooking times will vary depending on size. The flavours and textures here are well worth the effort. You certainly need a good hour of preparation, cooking and resting. Go on indulge yourself. Oh and someone else too!

Remove bird from packaging and allow to stand for 30 minutes. This allows any bag odours to subside. Meanwhile, finely chop the bacon, place into a food processor along with sage and a healthy grinding of pepper. Blitz until finely chopped and bound.

Starting at the neck cavity and using your fingers, slide them between the skin and the flesh, loosening the skin and creating a pocket over the breast meat. Take the bacon stuffing and force it into this pocket, spreading it out evenly using the palm of your hand. Do your utmost to keep skin intact.

For the bread sauce, put the milk and onion into a bowl over a pan of simmering water and slowly bring it to just below boiling point. The aim is to extract as much flavour from the onion and cloves, so the longer it takes the milk to boil, the stronger the flavour will be.

Remove the onion and whisk in the breadcrumbs until the sauce is thick and all the milk has been taken up. Keep the basin over the simmering water until the sauce is heated through. Season with a pinch of nutmeg, salt and pepper then finally stir in the butter. Set aside and keep warm.

To roast the bird, preheat the oven to 200°C (400°F). Heat a medium sized baking pan on the stove top to very hot. Add some oil and when hot, place bird in, on one side of the breast. Cook until golden, transfer to oven for 8 minutes then turn onto other side of the breast for another 8 minutes. Turn over, breast side up and bake for 6 minutes. By this time the bird should be almost cooked through. Remove from the oven and allow to rest for a further 8 minutes. The legs can be taken off straight away. Using a knife and a wad of paper towel to protect your hand from the heat, joint the legs by cutting in between the lower part of the breast and the thigh. Pierce with a knife and use your hand to dislocate the joint. You may need to use the knife to get through the tail end. Place legs back into oven for a further 5 minutes. They always need extra cooking.

Serves: 2

1 guinea fowl, approximately 1.2kg (2½lb)

120g (4¼ oz) bacon with at least 30% fat

5 fresh sage leaves

Cracked black pepper

Bread Sauce

500ml (16 fl oz) milk

1 small onion, studded with three cloves

110g (3¾ oz) fresh breadcrumbs

Nutmeg

Salt and freshly ground black pepper

30g (1 oz) butter

1 tsp butter, extra

1 tbs sugar

1 medium sized cooking apple, peeled and cut into a small dice

60ml (2 fl oz) Calvados (or brandy)

½ cup (125ml/4 fl oz) chicken stock

2 tbs chopped parsley

½ bunch watercress, picked and washed

To prepare the sauce, heat a medium sized pan. Add the extra butter, sugar and apple. Cook until golden. Deglaze the pan with the Calvados, being careful as it may ignite. For safety it's always best to remove pan from heat before adding the alcohol. Cook until evaporated, add the stock and cook until reduced by half. Add a pinch of salt and pepper, the chopped parsley and set aside.

Once bird has rested, proceed by carving the breast. Slice down either side of the breast bone using a sharp knife and following the ribs of the carcass. If for some reason the breast is not thoroughly cooked, place briefly into a hot pan. Once legs have had a little extra time in the oven, remove allow to cool then pull meat away from the bone and shred.

To serve, place a large spoonful of the bread sauce into the centre of a bowl, top with a small handful of watercress and the shredded leg meat. Top with breast and nap with sauce.

Note: If bread sauce seems on the thin side (sauce should not spread very much when put on a plate) add more crumbs, if it seems so firm that a spoon will stand up in it, add a little more milk.

OCEANELEMENTS

When I am not cooking, presenting, writing or producing you'll generally find me at the beach, surfing. I've always loved the ocean. It's a never-ending bounty of beautiful food, a place to relax, a place to exercise and a place I go to think.

I grew up on a dairy farm, where meat was the staple. The only seafood I saw was by catching yabbies in the dam, throwing a fishing line in the creek or going to the fish and chip shop which was a good hours drive away.

These days, I'm a regular at the Sydney Fish Market, where I am constantly amazed at the myriad creatures that come out of the sea. In fact over 100 species a day are auctioned at this market and a staggering 15,000 tonnes of seafood sold there annually.

Seafood is so good for us, packed with key long-chain omega 3 fatty acids which help prevent coronary heart disease. It's generally low in cholesterol and high in protein, vitamins and minerals.

This chapter will give you a good understanding of a few simple ways to make sure you can get 3 good serves of fish a week.

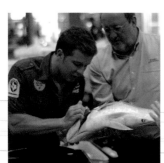

Whiting in a Bag

Cooking in a bag is a method that has been with us for many years. Although it's not commonly used, I enjoy doing it because when you open it at the table the aroma you have trapped in the bag is awesome and I save on washing up time. Most supermarkets stock oven bags these days but if not, use a buttered piece of aluminium foil instead. This is perfect for those eating alone.

The fish is basically steamed within the bag. It's such a healthy, low moisture option for cooking. All the goodness stays within the bag.

Serves: 1

1 zucchini, cut into batons
1 tomato, core removed and cut into wedges
5 olives
180g (6 ½ oz) whiting fillets
1 bay leaf
Salt and freshly ground black pepper
2 tbs extra virgin olive oil
1 lemon

Preheat oven to 220°C (430°F).

Place zucchini, tomato and olives into an oven bag. Top with the fish then the bay leaf and sprinkle lightly with salt and pepper. Drizzle with olive oil and tie bag.

Bake for 6 to 7 minutes, time may vary due to thickness of fish. The best way to test if done is by touch. It should be firm with a spring in the flesh when pressed.

Open bag and serve accompanied with a wedge of lemon.

"give me a fish, i eat for a day,
teach me to fish, i eat for a lifetime" robert louis stevenson.

Cassoulet of Blue Eye & Mussels

Serves: 2

300g (10 ½ oz) blue eye, skinned and free of bones

1 ½ tsp coarse sea salt

Mussels

30ml (1 fl oz) cooking oil

1 eschalot, finely sliced

1 bay leaf

few sprigs of thyme

½ tsp black peppercorns

75ml (2 ½ fl oz) dry white wine

10 mussels

Beans

100g (3 ½ oz) finely diced onion

40ml (1 ⅓ fl oz) olive oil

1 clove garlic, bruised

3 sprigs of fresh thyme

400g (14 oz) can cannellini beans, drained

Chicken stock or water

Breadcrumbs

1 cup (250ml/ 8 fl oz) olive oil

¼ loaf white bread, crusts removed and torn into small pieces

2 cloves garlic

5 sprigs fresh thyme

2 tomatoes peeled, deseeded and diced

3 tbs chopped flat or curly parsley

I am a lover of French cuisine and technique, I respect it immensely.

Everything from garlic sausage and pickled pork, to confit of duck, each region of France has its own interpretation. This particular dish, the cassoulet, is a dish that would normally take a few days to make. In this particular recipe, I have featured some of the basic elements, incorporated delicious seafood and taken a few days work out of it. Blue eye is a variety of fish, readily available in Australia. Feel free to substitute another firm fleshed fish maybe bass, hapuka or even kingfish.

Cut the blue eye into largish cubes, lightly salt and leave to cure for 20 minutes. After the 20 minutes, rinse under cold water and pat dry. Set aside until needed.

For the mussels, heat oil in a saucepan until a blue haze appears. Add the eschalot, bay leaf, thyme, peppercorns, wine and the mussels. Cover with a tight lid and cook for about 30 seconds. Lift the lid, remove mussels as they open and set aside. Strain the mussel liquid and reserve for the beans.

For the beans, sweat the onion in olive oil with the garlic and thyme, until soft and translucent. When soft, add the beans, reserved mussel stock and enough chicken stock or water to barely cover. Bring to the boil. When boiling, carefully remove a quarter of the beans with some of the liquid and puree in a blender until smooth. Return the mixture back to the beans.

For the breadcrumbs, heat oil and add breadcrumbs, garlic and thyme. Stir to help keep the colouring even and when golden, remove breadcrumbs from pan using a slotted spoon and drain on absorbent paper.

To serve, add the blue eye to the beans with tomatoes and parsley. Reheat gently for a few minutes; the blue eye should be firm but not dried out. Stir through the mussels in at the last minute; adjust seasoning with black pepper. Spoon into desired plates and scatter with freshly cooked breadcrumbs.

Crab Cakes

Here is a basic recipe for crab cakes. On occasion I have substituted fresh crab meat for tinned. I swear if you don't mention it to your guests, they won't notice. I have served them with Aioli (see Basic Mayonaise page 86).

Serves: 4

400g (14 oz) crab meat
125g (4 ½ oz) fresh white bread crumbs
5 tbs mayonnaise
3 tbs chopped parsley
3 tbs wholegrain mustard
1 tbs Worcestershire sauce
3 shallots, chopped
Juice of half a lemon

½ tsp cayenne pepper
3 tbs olive oil
salt and freshly ground black pepper
1 cup of picked watercress & lemon wedges, to serve

Mix all ingredients together except the oil and season with salt and pepper. Leave in the fridge for at least 20 minutes. With floured hands, very gently shape the mixture into small round patties. The less you handle them, the easier the job will be. As you shape each one, place it onto a floured plate.

Heat just enough olive oil to cover the bottom of a frying pan. When oil is hot, fry crab cakes, a few at a time being aware not to overcrowd the pan. Fry for two minutes on each side till golden. Serve on a bed of watercress with wedges of lemon and aioli.

Mussels in a Red Curry

Serves: 4

A big bowl of steaming hot mussels in a red hot curry after a long surf in the cooler months of winter can be my friend any day!

1kg (2lb) mussels in the shell

2 tsp olive oil

1 tbs red curry paste

200ml (6½ fl oz) coconut milk

1 tbs fish sauce

1 tbs brown sugar

5 to 6 fresh long red chillies, split in half lengthwise and seeds removed

½ cup coriander (cilantro) leaves, chopped

½ cup basil leaves

1 lime

Note: Always remember if they don't open during cooking, don't eat them.

Clean mussels under cold running water with a stiff brush to remove grit and beard. Set aside.

Heat a heavy based pan over a medium heat, add oil and curry paste and cook until fragrant. Add a little of the coconut milk and stir until paste has dissolved. Add fish sauce, sugar, remaining coconut milk and mussels and cover with a lid.

Steam the mussels until they have all opened, then remove with a slotted spoon and set aside. Check consistency of sauce, it should be quite viscous (thick). If too thin, continue cooking until thickened.

Toss in the chillies, coriander and basil leaves and cook for a minute. Squeeze in a little lime juice, add the mussels back, stir through and serve. Serve accompanied with a bowl of steamed rice (optional).

Cuttlefish Risotto

I love risotto; it's a great way to feed a few people from the one pan. This particular one highlights the uniqueness of using cuttlefish, a member of the cephalopod family. As you'll see, the dish is finished with yoghurt as opposed to Parmesan cheese. I won't go into it, rather you'll have to judge for yourself.

Serves: 4 to 6

1kg (2lb) small cuttlefish or squid (with ink sacs still intact)

1 tbs olive oil

1 clove garlic, sliced

Salt and freshly ground black pepper

1½ to 2 litres (2½ to 3½ pints) chicken stock

50g (1¾ oz) butter

1 onion, finely chopped

400g (14 oz) Arborio rice

125ml (4 fl oz) dry white wine

2 small red chillies, seeds removed and finely sliced

2 tbs natural yoghurt

½ cup fresh mint, torn

Release the ink sacs from the cuttlefish by removing the tentacles along with the stomach. The ink sac is a silver pouch found just between the eyes. Be gentle when removing, you don't want them to burst and set aside. Cut the tentacles away from the head and set aside. Slip the bone away from the middle of the cuttlefish and discard. (Also see the DVD for preparation of cuttlefish).

Rinse the tubes under cold water and then pat dry with kitchen paper.

Heat olive oil in a pan and add garlic. Season the cuttlefish tubes and tentacles with salt and pepper, add to pan and cook for 2 to 3 minutes until brown, turn and leave in pan until cooked. Remove and set aside.

Heat stock in a saucepan and keep at a gentle simmer. Melt the butter in a clean frying pan, add a splash of olive oil to prevent burning, then gently sauté onion till translucent. Turn up the heat and add the rice, stirring until the rice starts to crackle.

Pour in the white wine and cook until evaporated. Lower the heat and begin adding stock, a ladle at a time, stirring frequently. The idea is to add enough stock to keep the rice slightly nutty yet the grains plump, full and creamy. This takes approximately 20 minutes; it will vary depending on the rice.

Burst the ink sacs, I find the best way is to put them into a strainer and crush them with a back of a spoon, add to the risotto and stir in along with the chilli.

Just before serving, slice the cuttlefish and fold through the risotto with the yoghurt and mint leaves.

Note: These days you can buy pre-packaged "ink" which means a little less mess and a little less time consuming as it is not necessary to remove the ink sacs. For this particular dish you would use 2 heaped teaspoons of ink.

Garfish with Braised Peppers

Serves: 2

Fresh fillets of garfish, when lightly steamed would have to be one of the sweetest tasting little fish I have ever eaten. This marriage of soft sweet peppers with the bay leaf, star anise and garfish is worth every mouthful.

This dish is relatively simple to put together, however if garfish are not available try rouge or even monkfish if you can get a hold of it. I have rolled the garfish for presentation. Not all fish will roll like this.

1 medium onion, finely sliced

⅓ cup (80ml/ 2 ½ fl oz) olive oil

1 red capsicum (bell pepper)

1 yellow capsicum (bell pepper)

5 sprigs fresh thyme

1 bay leaf

1 clove garlic, bruised

1 star anise

100ml (3 fl oz) fish or chicken stock

30ml (1 fl oz) verjuice* (or white wine)

Sea salt and black pepper

¼ cup continental parsley, coarsely chopped

400g (14 oz) garfish fillets

6 small fingerling potatoes, steamed till tender

In a heavy-based pan, soften the onion in the olive oil over a gentle heat without colouring. Add the peppers, which have had the pith and seeds removed and been cut into 2cm (1 inch) squares.

Throw in the thyme sprigs, bay leaf, bruised garlic, star anise, stock and verjuice. Cover with a tight fitting lid and cook over low heat for approximately 25 minutes. Season with salt, pepper and parsley.

Place the fish fillets on top of the braised peppers along with the steamed potatoes. Cover with a piece of parchment paper to stop moisture loss and cook on a gentle heat for a further 4 to 5 mins depending on the thickness of the fish. Serve immediately.

*Verjuice is unfermented green grape juice.

Oysters

I only really started eating oysters over the last 5 years. Before that I thought they were totally gross and I could not fathom eating one let alone a half dozen, but they grow on you. They are rich and silky smooth. Some people like to swallow them whole, but I like to sink my teeth into them at least twice before swallowing.

I love eating them natural, maybe with a crack of black pepper and a hint of lime or lemon. My favourites differ depending where in the world you are. Currently I am living in Sydney, Australia and the Coffin Bay oysters from the cooler waters of South Australia are incredibly moreish, these are definitely an aphrodisiac.

I have given a few different dressings to whet your appetite. Each recipe is designed for a dozen oysters. Citrus Vinaigrette is also another wonderful option, see page 207.

Serves: Each sauce
12 oysters

Oysters with Red Wine Vinegar and Eschalot

3 eschalots, finely diced

100ml (3 fl oz) red wine vinegar (Forvum Cabernet Sauvignon)

Cracked black pepper

Mix eschalot and vinegar together and let stand for 10 minutes before serving spooned over oysters. Finish with cracked black pepper.

Oysters with Red Chilli Nahm Jim

1 clove garlic

1 long red chilli, seeds removed

1 red birds eye chilli

1 coriander (cilantro) root

A pinch sea salt

30g (1 oz) palm or brown sugar

100ml (3 fl oz) lime juice

30ml (1 fl oz) fish sauce

Crisp fried eschalots or onion

Fresh coriander (cilantro) leaves, to serve

In a mortar and pestle pound the garlic, chillies and coriander root along with sea salt to a paste. Add sugar and pound again until smooth. Add lime juice and fish sauce; give a quick mix and taste. Like most south east Asian food it should be a good balance of sweet, sour and salty with the addition of spice. When ready to serve, nap over each oyster and top with crisp fried eschalot and coriander leaves.

Oysters Natural with Brown Bread and Watercress Sandwiches

1 lemon, cut into wedges

2 tbs butter

6 slices brown bread

1 cup watercress leaves

Salt and freshly ground black pepper

This is a simple way of serving oysters. Buttered brown bread with watercress, salt and pepper, served alongside a few oysters and a glass of champagne is a match made in heaven.

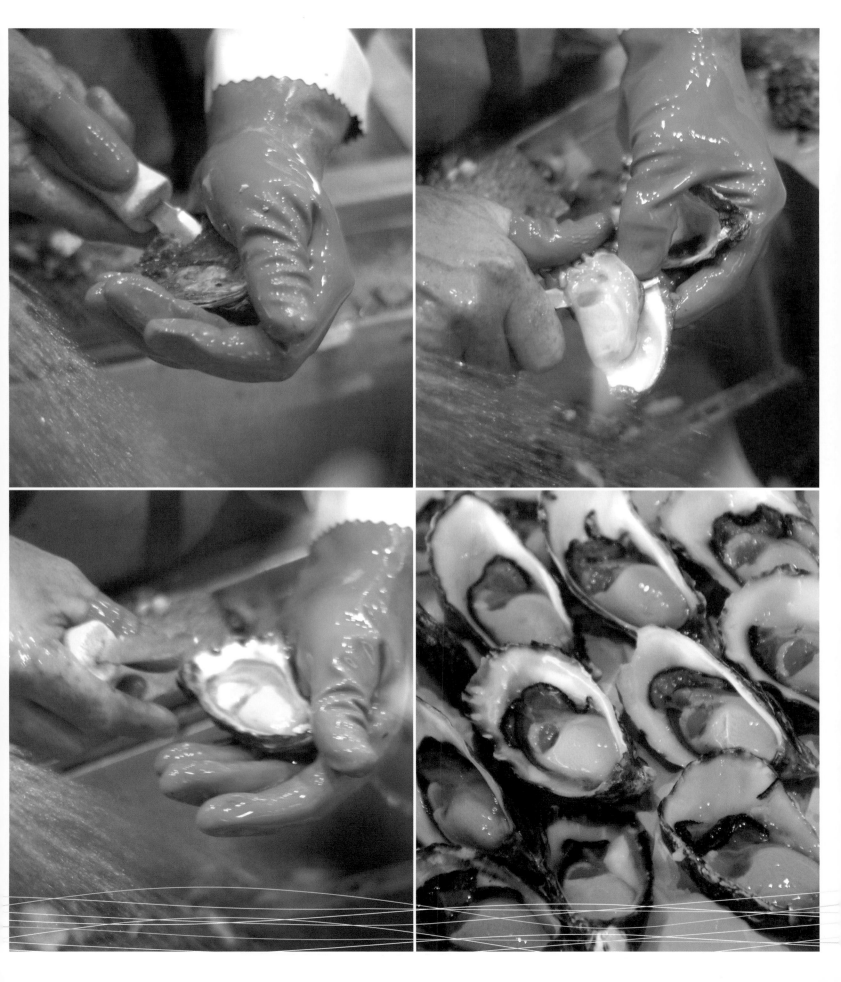

Pan Roasted Barramundi with White Asparagus & Citrus Vinaigrette

Serves: 2

When it comes to Australian fish, you won't find anything more native than the barramundi, it's sweet, firm flesh is a meal worth remembering.

This dish will work well with most firm, white, fleshed fish particularly, monk fish, black bass and whiting.

2 barramundi fillets, skin & bones removed
(approximately 200g/7 oz)
Salt and freshly ground black pepper
Olive oil
6 spears white asparagus

Note: Because fish comes in all different shapes and sizes it's important to remember that cooking times will differ from
fish to fish. The best way to tell if your fish is cooked through is to push a skewer or a small
knife into the flesh, if it comes out with no resistance then fish is cooked.

To cook your piece of fish to perfection, try taking it out of the pan a minute or so early and allowing it to rest. This basically means to keep cooking without the heat of the pan. This will also stop it from drying out.

Season the fish with salt and pepper. Heat a heavy based pan over a medium high heat till a blue haze appears in the pan.

Gently lay fish into the pan, serving side down. Lower the heat to medium and cook the fish for a few minutes until golden. Turn the fish and cook through.

Blanch the asparagus in plenty of boiling salted water till tender (approximately 3 minutes). Remove from boiling water and refresh under cold running water. Serve fish on top of asparagus, napped with citrus vinaigrette.

Serves: 8

Citrus Vinaigrette

Any leftover citrus vinaigrette will keep for up to 4 days.

1 ruby grapefruit

1 orange

2 limes

⅓ cup (80ml/2½ fl oz) olive oil

2 tbs red wine vinegar

1 tsp soy sauce

1 tsp pink peppercorns

¼ bunch coriander (cilantro), finely chopped

Salt and freshly ground black pepper

Remove the skin and pith from all citrus. Segment the fruit, separating flesh from pith using a small paring knife.

Squeeze remaining juice from the core of the citrus into a bowl. Finely dice the segments and add to the juice, along with remaining ingredients.

Mix well, season with salt and pepper.

If a little sharp, add more oil, and if too oily add a little more vinegar.

Salt Crust Salmon

Served with a warm salad of kipfler potato, oven-dried tomatoes, watercress and a Fine Herb Mayonnaise (see page 86).

Serves: Yields about 8 to 10 main course portions.

The Salt Crust

1kg (2.2lb) coarse cooking salt

1kg (2.2lb) flour (plain)

650ml (20 fl oz) water

The Salmon

1 whole salmon (approximately 2½ to 3kg / 5½ to 6½ lb) this should yield about 10 main course portions

Reserved stalks from the herb mayonnaise (see page 86)

Sea salt and cracked black pepper

10 Roma tomatoes

3 tsp fresh or dried thyme leaves

30 small steamed kipfler potatoes

1 bunch fresh watercress

Note: If the salmon is too big for your oven, remove head and tail to fit.

To prepare salt crust; knead salt, flour and water together to form a smooth dough and allow to rest for 1 hour wrapped in an old shopping bag or plastic wrap. No need to refridgerate.

To prepare the salmon; trim the fins and tail with scissors to eliminate piercing the crust. Push herbs and seasoning into the cavity of the fish.

Roll out the salt crust to approximately 8mm (⅓ inch) thick. It should be wide enough to fold over and wrap salmon completely, leaving no holes.

Place onto a preheated baking tray (260°C/500°F). Bake salmon for 20 to 25 minutes, remove and allow to rest for 10 minutes before breaking the crust. Break the crust, open flap and let rest another 15 minutes before serving.

To serve, place a portion of the salmon over top of potatoes, semi-dried tomatoes and watercress. Nap with the Fine Herb Mayonnaise.

To prepare semi-dried tomatoes; simply halve tomatoes and place into a baking dish in a single layer. Sprinkle with thyme leaves, douse with olive oil and season with salt and cracked black pepper. Place in a low oven (150°C/300°F) for about 1 to 1½ hours till slightly wilted and fragrant.

Scallop Ceviche

Serves: 8

Two words – 'fresh scallops'. This dish is based on the scallops being super fresh; without that sea-blessed flavour this dish is pointless. This is absolutely decadent, rich and very fresh. I call it white caviar. I have served it with Avocado Salsa (see page 89) on toasted tortilla chips.

1 large flour tortilla
2 tbs olive oil
150g (5⅓ oz) scallops, roe removed
2 tbs hazelnut or olive oil
½ tsp crushed, roasted coriander seeds
Squeeze of lime juice
Pinch sea salt and freshly cracked black pepper
Coriander (cilantro) sprigs (optional)

To prepare the tortilla chips, start by folding the tortilla in half. Cut into long thin triangles. Place onto an oven tray, brush with a little olive oil, sprinkle lightly with sea salt and bake in the oven at 180°C (350°F) for 10 minutes or until crisp and golden.

With a clean sharp knife, cut the scallops into small 4 mm (⅛th inch) dice and place into a chilled, clean bowl. Moisten with the hazelnut oil and sprinkle with coriander seed. This can be prepared up to 3 hours prior to serving.

Five minutes before serving, squeeze in the lime juice along with a hint of salt and pepper.

To serve place a small spoonful of the avocado salsa then a spoonful of the scallop onto the tortilla chips. Garnish with a sprig of coriander.

Shen's Singapore Chilli Mud Crab

This is a great recipe from my friend Shen Tan in Singapore. Nothing better on a hot night in Singapore than sitting out under the stars eating this dish.

Serves: 2

1 fresh mud crab (approximately 700g/1½ lb)

80ml (2½ fl oz) vegetable oil

5 eschalots, finely chopped

4 cloves garlic, finely chopped

2cm (¾ inch) knob ginger, finely chopped

2 long red chillies, finely chopped

1 stalk curry leaves (optional)

2 tomatoes, chopped

2 tbs sweet chilli sauce

2 tbs tomato sauce/ketchup

½ tbs light soy sauce

Large pinch of salt

1 tsp sugar

1 tbs vinegar

White pepper, to taste

1 tsp sesame oil

½ cup (125ml/4 fl oz) chicken stock

2 tsp cornflour

1 egg, beaten

3 green shallots, finely sliced on the angle

*Please contact your local animal welfare/protection agency or humane society for the correct procedure in your country to anaesthetise your crab. In Australia, this information is listed on the RSPCA website.
See also the segment on crab preparation on the DVD.

To prepare the crab it is important to anesthetise it first*. I find the most humane and safest way is to place it into a freezer for a good hour and a half. After this time the crab is still. Proceed to spike it through the head to sever the nerves. Separate the carapace (shell) from the body to remove the yellowy grey gills and spongy parts. Hit the legs and larger front nippers with the back of a knife or the flat side of a cleaver to crack the shell. This is to make the eating process easier.

In a wok or large pot over high heat, fry the crab in half of the olive oil until it turns red (approximately 3 to 4 minutes), remove and set aside. Add remaining oil and fry the eschalot, garlic, ginger, chilli and curry leaves (optional) till fragrant. Add tomato and fry till soft.

Mix together the sweet chilli sauce, tomato sauce, light soy sauce, salt, sugar, vinegar, white pepper, sesame oil and chicken stock, and set aside.

Return crab to the wok along with half of the sweet chilli sauce mixture, stir fry for 2 minutes then add the remainder of the sauce.

Blend cornflour with 60ml/2 fl oz water until smooth. Add to sauce with egg and stir until thickened. Serve crab topped with chopped shallots, accompanied with steamed rice.

Steamed Clams with Sausage

Serves: 2

This is a wonderful variation of the Portuguese dish "Alentjana".

So tasty and simple and will always go down well with a glass of dry white wine.

Keep in mind if small clams are not available, use mussels or cockles.

2 tbs olive oil
250g (9 oz) Chorizo sausage, finely diced
2 cloves garlic, finely sliced
1 small hot red chilli
30 small clams
120ml (4 fl oz) dry white wine
400g (14 oz) can peeled tomatoes
¼ cup chopped parsley

215

Note: If the clams don't open up whilst cooking, don't eat them.

Heat oil in a heavy-based pan (you need to have a lid). When a blue haze appears above the pan add the sausage and cook until golden.

Add garlic and chilli and cook for 30 seconds then add the clams along with the white wine. Cover with lid.

Steam the clams until all have opened, approximately 2 minutes. When opened add the tomatoes and chopped parsley. Heat through, season with a little salt and pepper and serve.

Thai Fish Salad

This is the sort of salad you can prepare in minimal time, looks impressive and is loaded with protein and omega fatty acids.

Serves: 2

If green mango is unavailable substitute green papaya, and if that fails add some ruby grapefruit segments roughly chopped.

1 tbs olive oil
200g (7oz) fresh kingfish, skin and bones removed
1 small red chilli, finely chopped
1 clove garlic
1 tbs palm sugar
2 limes
1 tbs fish sauce
A handful of bean sprouts
2 large red chillies, seeds removed and finely sliced
2 small green mangoes, peeled, sliced and finely shredded
(the French call it julienne)
½ bunch mint leaves
½ bunch coriander (cilantro) leaves
½ handful, crisp fried Asian shallots*

216

Heat oil in a pan till a blue haze appears. Add kingfish and brown on both sides for a couple of minutes. Now depending on how thick the fish is, will determine on how cooked your piece of fish is.

In a mortar and pestle, (a big heavy bowl looking thing with a heavy short stick for crushing food stuffs) add the chopped chilli, garlic and palm sugar. Crush to a paste. Add the lime juice and fish sauce. Taste it, it should be good. If the flavours are a little unbalanced, add a little more chilli or palm sugar to your liking.

After the kingfish has had a few minutes to rest, slice it thinly, place into a large mixing bowl, along with remaining ingredients and dressing. Mix lightly and serve.

*Usually available in the Asian food section of your supermarket.

Tuna Carpaccio with White Radish & Pistachio

Serves: 2

I love raw tuna, what more do I need to tell you? This dish speaks for itself. If white radishes are unavailable, then try some thin slices of raw Jerusalem artichoke.

1 small white radish (daikon)
200g (7 oz) tuna
2 tbs pistachio oil, or extra virgin olive oil
1 lime
1 tbs roasted pistachio nuts, chopped
1 punnet mustard cress
Fresh chervil to garnish (optional)
Sea salt flakes and cracked black pepper

Peel and finely slice the radish paper thin either with a very sharp knife or preferably with a mandolin. Lay flat in a circular bed on a plate.

With a sharp knife slice the tuna across the grain as thinly as you possibly can. When choosing a piece of tuna look for something with minimal sinew, it makes for better slicing and eating.

Layer the tuna over the sliced radish and douse with the pistachio oil and a squeeze of the lime juice. Scatter with the nuts, mustard cress, chervil, sea salt and cracked black pepper.

Boudin Blanc of Salmon with Fennel Vinaigrette

This dish is a reflection of my time at Bistro Moncur. Not necessarily a simple recipe, but well worth the effort. Such refined textures and flavours.

This is the sort of dish to tackle when you're trying to impress and have more than twenty minutes up your sleeve.

Cut fish into 2cm (1 inch) pieces. Place into a large, cold bowl with egg and salt. Now place that bowl over another filled with iced water. Mix ingredients until well combined.

Transfer the mixture to a food processor and puree until smooth and glutenous in texture. If doubling the quantity be sure to puree the fish in 2 batches, this will stop fish from becoming warm.

Return fish puree to the bowl over the ice and slowly work in the cream. Season with pepper, nutmeg and a touch more salt, if needed. Add the chopped chervil.

Place mixture into a piping bag, no nozzle is needed and pipe a sausage shape about 15cm (6 inches) long onto a piece of cling film. Fold the flap of plastic over the mixture and tuck under. Roll the mixture to form a sausage shape. Twist the ends, one at a time, pushing out any air pockets and tie to form a tight sausage.

Prepare a pot of water, by bringing up to 80°C (175°) over a medium heat, when temperature is reached (steaming but not boiling) place the Boudin in and poach for approximately 8 to 10 minutes until firm, then refresh in iced water, if not using immediately.

To serve, remove plastic, lay over a bed of celery batons and watercress and nap with the fennel vinaigrette.

Fennel Vinaigrette

In a saucepan, sweat eschalots and fennel seeds in olive oil until eschalots are translucent. Add tomato essence and verjuice, bring to the boil and then reduce to a simmer for 5 minutes. Remove from heat, throw in basil leaves and leave for 20 minutes before straining. Season with salt and pepper.

*Verjuice is unfermented green grape juice.

220

Serves: 4

The Boudin of Salmon

300g (10 ½ oz) salmon flesh, skin and bones removed

1 egg

6g (¼ oz) salt

300ml (9 ½ fl oz) cream

White pepper

Nutmeg

7g (¼ oz) chopped chervil

Celery batons and watercress

Fennel vinaigrette

3 eschalots, peeled and sliced

15g (½ oz) fennel seeds

120ml (4 fl oz) olive oil

60ml (2 fl oz) tomato essence (the juice of a strained, crushed tomato)

50ml (1 ½ fl oz) verjuice* or 1 tbs of white balsamic vinegar

A few basil leaves, torn

Salt & pepper

Note: Emulsification: everything will emulsify better over ice.
Any utensils used should be refrigerated before use, i.e. bowls, spoons, processor attachments.

pastoralelements

I look back at my life growing up on the farm and consider myself one of the lucky ones. Not just because of the wide-open spaces and the sense of unrestricted freedom, but the satisfaction of being independent and resourceful.

We were dairy farmers, but we also grew our own beef cattle, kept a few pigs as well as the odd sheep. We relied upon the elements for our resources. Rain, hail or shine, there was always meat on the table.

I guess over the years I've come to understand the need for a healthy and balanced lifestyle. That's why a moderate amount of red meat finds its way onto my menu at least 3 or 4 times a week. Whether it's a juicy steak or a helping of Pat's Pasta Sauce.

And besides… the nutritional facts back it up. Iron for energy and concentration, protein for growth and repair, zinc to promote a healthy immune system, Vitamin B to maintain the nervous system and Omega 3 to sustain a healthy heart.

So go on, sink your teeth into a piece of meat and enjoy the pastoral elements.

Beef with Almonds & Green Olives

I was fortunate enough to be given this recipe on my way to work one day by a Spanish taxi driver. I don't remember his name or even the cab company he worked for, but I thank him for this wonderful meal. It really is worth the time and effort. Oyster blade is the way to go, it is my favourite cut of meat, you can't beat that sticky residue it leaves on your lips after having braised it slowly for a couple of hours, YUM.

Serves: 4

1.2kg (2½ lb) braising beef
(I suggest oyster blade)

Salt and freshly ground black pepper

50ml (1½ fl oz) olive oil

50ml (1½ fl oz) brandy

2 medium onions, quartered

2 large tomatoes (blanched, refreshed and skinned), quartered

100g (3½ oz) blanched almonds
(cut into splinters)

100g (3½ oz) green olives

2 cloves garlic

400ml (12¾ fl oz) red wine
(pinot noir)

1.5 to 2 litres (2½ to 3½ pints) beef stock

Trim the beef of any visible fat and cut into large cubes approximately 3cm (1 inch). Leave any sinew, as this will break down and become very gelatinous in the slow braising process. Lightly season with salt and pepper and brown in a heavy based braising pan, using the olive oil.

When the meat is browned all over, deglaze the pan with the brandy; be careful as it is likely to ignite. When alcohol has reduced, add onion, tomato, almonds and olives. Add the whole cloves of garlic, red wine and enough stock to cover. Bring to the boil.

Turn off heat and seal the braising pan with either a lid or some parchment paper to stop moisture from being lost. Place into the oven at 140°C (285°F) for approximately 1½ to 2 hours. The meat should basically have no resistance when pierced with a skewer.

Skim any visible fat from the cooking liquid with a ladle as this will cloud the beautiful characteristics of both the wine and meat. The best way to serve this is to finish with seasoning, chopped fresh parsley and a helping of mashed potato (see page 121) or buttered pasta on the side.

Blanquette of Veal

Serves: 4

Basically a white veal stew. The thing I appreciate most about this dish is not just the simplicity of something that is so luscious and velvety in texture, but the whole slow sensuous braise of a tough piece of meat to reveal something so ethereal.

1kg (2.2lb) veal shoulder or leg meat (bone removed)

50g (1¾ oz) butter

12 baby onions

2 tbs olive oil

80g (2¾ oz) plain flour

1 litre (1¾ pints) boiling chicken stock

White pepper

Nutmeg

12 baby carrots, peeled and blanched

12 small new potatoes, steamed

1 cup fresh peas (frozen will do if unavailable)

Chopped parsley

Cream

If the joint of meat you have purchased still has the bone intact, use a sharp knife to remove it from the meat. Trim any thick fat and skin and cut into 3cm (1 inch) cubes.

In a heavy based pan, melt the butter and add the onions and olive oil and sweat until transparent. Add meat and cook until the meat has changed colour but not browned.

Sift in flour and mix well. Cook the flour without browning for a couple of minutes.

Slowly incorporate stock until all is absorbed. Season with pepper and nutmeg, cover with parchment paper and braise for approximately 1 hour 40 minutes, stirring occasionally. The meat is ready when tender and has lost its resistance when a skewer or a small knife is pushed into it.

Just before serving, finish with steamed carrots, potatoes and peas. Work in the parsley and a small amount of cream. Finish by seasoning with salt and freshly ground pepper.

Grilled Sirloin Steak with Herb Crust

This crust works well with beef, chicken or fish. Once made, it will keep perfectly well in the freezer for up to 2 months. It always looks impressive when served; in fact I would be surprised if you don't get the occasional WOW when served over the top of your favourite piece of flesh.

The Crust

100g (3 ½ oz) butter
100g (3 ½ oz) fresh breadcrumbs (brioche crumbs if you can get them)
100g (3 ½ oz) Gruyere cheese
50g (1¾ oz) basil, chopped
50g (1¾ oz) curly parsley, chopped
1 tbs Worcestershire sauce
Cracked black pepper

Place all ingredients in a food processor and process until smooth and homogenous. Remove from the processor and place onto a sheet of greaseproof (silicone) paper. Cover with a second sheet of paper. Roll flat to 3mm (⅛th inch) thick. Chill for 10 minutes before cutting to desired size. Generally the size of whatever you're serving it on.

The Steak

2 x 220g (7¾ oz) sirloin steaks
Salt and freshly ground black pepper
1 tbs olive oil

Season steak with salt and pepper. Cook for 4 to 6 minutes each side on a griddle pan or until cooked to your liking. Remove steaks and rest for 3 to 4 minutes.

Top each steak with a piece of the rolled herb crust that has been cut to the same size as the steak. Place under a preheated grill until crust has lightly browned. Remove from grill and serve immediately alongside a helping of grilled mushrooms.

Serves: Herb Crust - 8

Note: Grilled mushrooms: Season mushrooms with a little olive oil. salt & pepper. Place under pre-heated grill, cook for 2 tc 3 minutes on either side until tender.

Serves: 2

228

Quick, Easy Lamb & Black Bean Stir-fry

Serves: 2

This is a great stir-fry for beginners considering there's not too much involved. It's great for those on the run and certainly low in carbohydrates. The most important thing to remember when stir-frying is that the wok needs to be hot so you are searing the food, not stewing.

These days most good supermarkets will stock a lot of the Asian convenience items I have used in this dish.

1 tbs olive oil
300g (10 ½ oz) lamb loin, thinly sliced
1 clove garlic, finely chopped
1 medium onion, thinly sliced
2 stalks celery, leaves trimmed and thinly sliced on an angle
1 tsp cornflour, optional
¼ cup (60ml/ 2 fl oz)) black bean sauce
1 tsp teriyaki sauce
To garnish - 2 red chilli's deseeded and sliced,
2 green shallots finely sliced at an angle

Heat olive oil in a wok or large frying pan. Combine lamb and garlic and stir-fry in 2 batches until meat is well browned. Remove from the wok and set aside.

Stir-fry onion and celery. Blend cornflour with black bean sauce and teriyaki sauce in a small bowl. Return meat to the wok, add sauce mixture and stir until mixture boils and thickens. Serve with boiled rice, topped with chilli and shallots.

Lamb Cutlets with Crushed Peas

Love my lamb; love it even more when it's cooked in a matter of minutes.

Serves: 1

1 tbs olive oil
1 clove garlic, finely sliced
3 x 60g (2 oz) lamb cutlets
Salt and freshly ground black pepper
½ cup (60g/ 2 oz) frozen peas
1 tsp butter
1 tbs olive oil
Pinch of nutmeg
Wedge of lemon

Heat olive oil in a medium sized fry pan along with the sliced garlic, being careful not to burn it. Season cutlets with salt and pepper, add to pan and cook for 2-3 minutes on each side until cooked to your liking. Remove and set aside to rest for a couple of minutes.

To prepare the mushy peas, heat the peas in a saucepan with 3 tbs of water. Cover with a lid and heat till steam appears. Turn off heat. Add butter, olive oil and a pinch each of salt, pepper and nutmeg. Crush with a fork. Keep warm. Serve the lamb cutlets along side the mushy peas with a wedge of lemon.

Quick Meat & 3 Veg

Serves: 1

I crave meals like this, really simple yet high in vitamins and minerals.

Perfect for those working late and needing something quick, nutritious and portion controlled.

80g (3 oz) broccolini (broccoli is also fine)
3 spears asparagus, stems trimmed and peeled
5 cherry tomatoes, halved
3 tbs olive oil
180g (6½ oz) beef fillet
Salt and freshly ground black pepper
1 tsp butter
Lemon

235

Place vegetables into a thick-based saucepan and cover with ½ cup (125ml/ 4 fl oz) water and 2 tbs of the olive oil. Set over a medium to high heat, cover and bring to the boil. When the lid starts to flutter, remove from heat and set aside, leaving covered.

Cut the fillet into thin slices about 3mm (⅛th inch). Season liberally with salt and pepper. Heat the remaining olive oil and butter in a heavy-based fry pan until butter starts to foam. Add meat slices and brown for 30 - 40 seconds on both sides. Serve steak with vegetables and a cheek of lemon (optional).

Rare Roasted Spicy Italian Beef Fillet

Sometimes for lunch or dinner, I will prepare a mix of say 3 or 4 simple dishes
that we can pick at. This is one that will get cooked more often than not. You
could serve this as an individual salad if you feel like it. I serve it along side a
couple of simple vegetable dishes.

Serves: 4

3 cloves garlic, roughly chopped
1 tbs fennel seeds
¼ tsp chilli flakes
½ tsp salt
2 tbs olive oil
750g (1½ lb) piece eye fillet, trimmed and tied
2 heads of witlof, leaves separated
100g (3½ oz) shaved Parmesan cheese
Extra virgin olive oil

Place garlic, fennel seeds, chilli and salt into a mortar and pestle and pound to a
paste (otherwise grind spices in a spice grinder or blender). Add oil to make a
pliable mixture. Rub into the beef and set aside to marinate for 20 minutes.

Preheat oven to 150°C (300°F). Heat a medium frypan to hot. Sear the beef on
all sides. Transfer to a baking tray, drop the oven temperature to 120°C (250°F)
and roast for 50 minutes. Remove from oven and set aside to rest 20 minutes
before slicing.

Slice beef and serve at room temperature with witlof leaves, shaved Parmesan,
a little extra dried chilli and a good splash of extra virgin olive oil.

Roast Fillet of Venison in a Green Waistcoat

Serves: 2

I am big fan of game meat, but it is a little trickier to cook. The lean cuts of meat like the loin and fillet tend to be very lean and therefore dry out and over cook if not nurtured. The extremity cuts like the shoulder, leg etc seem to be very sinewy and therefore need a lot of love, attention and slow cooking. Here's a recipe that highlights the nurturing of a succulent piece of fillet with a little extra insulation. Yum.

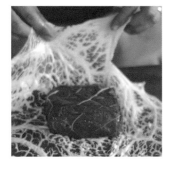

400g (14oz) piece venison fillet

1 tbs olive oil

5 sprigs of fresh thyme, leaves removed & stems discarded

½ tsp ground pimento (also known as allspice)

Black pepper

3-4 large silverbeet or spinach leaves (enough to wrap the fillet)

Caul fat (if not available use 5-6 thinly sliced pieces prosciutto)*

6 brown eschalots, peeled

8 baby carrots, scrubbed

6 baby turnips, scrubbed

A pinch of sugar

A little extra olive oil

2 tbs red wine vinegar

1 cup (250ml/ 8 fl oz) chicken stock

Salt

Trim any silver sinew from the fillet. Place oil, thyme leaves, pimento and a good grinding of black pepper onto a plate. Roll the fillet in the marinade and set aside.

Blanch the silverbeet in boiling water for 5 seconds to soften, then refresh in ice-cold water. Squeeze dry and lay out over a flat surface. Lay fillet over silverbeet and roll up leaving no spaces. Roll firmly in the stretched out caul fat. This will help to insulate the meat.

In a medium sized pan, brown the vegetables in a little extra oil with a pinch of sugar. When golden brown deglaze the pan with the vinegar, add stock and cook over a gentle heat until tender, approximately 8-10 minutes. When tender, season with a little salt and pepper, they should be quite peppery.

Heat a large pan with a touch of oil, when a blue haze appears above the pan, lay in the wrapped fillet. Cook over a medium heat until golden brown, approximately 5 minutes then turn and cook for a further 5 minutes. Remove from pan and rest for 5 minutes before carving.

To serve, scoop vegetables out in equal portioned sizes onto plates. Remember to carve venison across the grain (carving through the narrower width). Lay slices over vegetables, check sauce for seasoning one more time then nap over venison.

*Caul fat is an edible membrane, surrounding the intestines of animals. I have used a pork caul fat for this recipe, which can generally be purchased through a good butcher.

Roast Leg of Lamb Provencal Style

When I know I have a group of hungry footy players over for dinner, nine times out of ten they will eat leg of lamb. Here's a recipe I have been putting together of late. If you can get yourself a good blend of Provencal herbs, it can really make a difference. The herb mix I am using at the moment has thyme, marjoram, parsley, tarragon and lavender in it; it's out of this world.

Serves: 4 to 6

Note: Cooking time will vary depending on the size of leg of lamb. Add an extra 10 minutes cooking time per 500g (1lb).

1 tsp coarse sea salt

2 cloves garlic

1 tbs Provencal herbs (or mixed Italian herbs)

½ tsp ground black pepper

2 tbs dry white wine

2 tbs olive oil

1 leg of lamb, with bone approximately 2kg (4½ lb)

Pound together the salt and one clove of garlic in a mortar and pestle*. Add herbs and pepper and pound to a paste. Mix in the white wine and olive oil.

Trim the leg of lamb of all skin and excess fat. Rub leg with the marinade, wrap in plastic and leave for an hour to allow the meat to absorb the flavours. Preheat oven to 190°C (375°F).

Heat a large roasting pan and brown the meat on all sides. Place into the oven for 20 minutes, turn over and cook for another 20 minutes before pulling out of the oven to rest, covered for a further 10 minutes with aluminum foil.

*If you don't have a mortar and pestle, on a chopping board, finely chop the garlic then add salt and crush with the heel of the knife to form a paste. Place into a small bowl and add remaining ingredients.

Roasted Potatoes

700g (1½ lb) kipfler or other waxy potatoes

1 whole bulb of garlic, broken into cloves with skin on

2 large sprigs of rosemary

3 tbs olive oil

Good pinch of salt and freshly ground black pepper

Wash the potatoes and if large, split into halves. Place into a baking tray with garlic cloves, rosemary, doused in olive oil and seasoned. Roast at 190°C (375°F) for approximately 40 minutes or until golden and tender.

Shaking Beef

Serves: 4

This is a Vietnamese dish that derives its name from the term "sauté". The pan is shaken as you would when sautéing. Another good reason to pull the wok out of the pantry and dust it off.

1 tbs fish sauce

1 tbs light soy sauce

2 cloves garlic, crushed

2 tsp sugar

600g (1⅓ lbs) good quality beef rump, cubed

1 bunch of watercress, washed and picked over

1 red onion, thinly sliced

⅓ cup mint leaves

2 tbs olive oil

Dressing:

1½ tbs lime juice

1 tbs fish sauce

1 tsp brown sugar

1 fresh red chilli, sliced

Place fish sauce, soy sauce, garlic and sugar in a bowl. Add beef cubes and toss. Set aside to marinate for an hour or two.

Arrange watercress, onion and mint on a platter. Mix dressing ingredients together in a large bowl.

Heat olive oil in a wok or large frying pan. Add beef and cook, shaking the pan to ensure the cubes are browned on all sides but still rare in the middle. Remove, add to dressing and toss well. Serve beef on top of salad ingredients.

Stir-fried Szechuan Beef with White Asparagus

Another one pan wonder! If Szechwan peppercorns are unavailable, substitute with ground star anise.

Serves: 2

250g (9 oz) tender beef (rump or sirloin)

1 tsp Szechuan peppercorns (lightly roasted and crushed to a powder)

1 tbs fish sauce

2 tbs olive oil

3 cloves garlic, thinly sliced

6 spears white asparagus, blanched until tender and cooled

7 spears fresh green asparagus, finely sliced

40ml (1⅓ fl oz) sweet chilli sauce

1 lime

1 long red chilli, deseeded and finely sliced

½ cup fresh mint leaves

½ cup fresh coriander leaves

Slice the meat into thin bite-sized pieces. Place into a bowl with ground pepper and fish sauce. Mix and allow to sit for ten minutes before cooking.

Heat oil in a wok and fry garlic until golden. Add beef and stir-fry for 30 seconds. Toss in asparagus and continue stir-frying.

Add sweet chilli sauce and a squeeze of lime juice. Remove from heat, add fresh chilli and herbs and serve.

T-bone Steak with Rosemary & Anchovy Sauce

Serves: 2

The T-bone steak to me is not the greatest piece of meat to cook, for the simple reason you have a piece or fillet and a piece of loin in the same cut. The fillet will generally cook quicker than the loin, leaving the meat unevenly cooked. However, I have fond memories of being a child holding a mammoth T-bone steak in both hands and being as happy as a pig in mud, with meat juices smeared from ear to ear.

Olive oil

2 x 350g (12½ oz) T-bone steaks, remember that at least 100g (3½ oz) of that is bone

Salt and freshly ground black pepper

In a large skillet or griddle pan, heat the olive oil until a blue haze appears.

Season the meat with both salt and pepper and lay into the hot pan. Cook until golden (approximately 3 minutes), then turn. Obviously depending on the thickness of the meat and the degree to which you like it cooked, determines how long it stays in the pan.

Once cooked to your liking, remove from pan and rest for 5 minutes before serving. Douse in anchovy and rosemary sauce and accompany with steamed green beans (optional).

247

Serves: 2

Anchovy & Rosemary Sauce

6 salted anchovy fillets

2 cloves garlic

1 tbs fresh rosemary leaves, chopped

Juice of 1 lemon

80ml (2½ fl oz) extra virgin olive oil

With the addition of a pinch of salt, pound the anchovies, garlic and rosemary in a mortar and pestle. Slowly add the lemon juice, stirring to blend. Finally add the olive oil in a thin stream, stirring continuously.

Thai Style Pork & Eggplant Curry

I love everything there is to love about Thai food; it's simplicity of preparation and complexity of flavours.

The balance of sweet, sour and salty varies from region to region, as does the use of chilli. Have a go at this one; adjust flavouring to your taste. A little more lime juice here and a little more palm sugar there.

1 large tbs red curry paste

375ml (12 fl oz) can coconut cream

3cm (1 inch) knob ginger, peeled and finely sliced

5 kaffir lime leaves

2 tbs fish sauce

1 tbs palm sugar

2 limes

6 golf ball sized eggplant, halved

1 cup of pea eggplants

350g (12½ oz) pork fillet, finely sliced

steamed rice, to serve

1 cup bean sprouts

2 tbs fried shallots

A handful of fresh Thai basil

Serves: 2

Note: Eggplant can be substituted for green beans, snow peas, pumpkin or zucchini.

Fry the curry paste in a third of the coconut cream in a saucepan. Cook for a few minutes, until the cream 'cracks' or splits and the curry paste is aromatic.

Add ginger, 3 of the lime leaves and remaining coconut cream. Bring to the boil, stir in the fish sauce and palm sugar and squeeze in lime juice.

Add eggplant and pork. Bring to the boil and simmer for 1 minute. Serve with steamed rice, topped with bean sprouts, crispy shallots, the remaining 2 lime leaves finely shredded, and basil.

Whole Roasted Leg of Lamb Stuffed with Garlic & Rosemary

Serves: 4 to 6

Here's another delicious way to prepare a leg of lamb.

For carving purposes, I find it easier to remove the H bone first. This is the bone that connects the leg to the carcase, not all legs will have one. It will depend on whether or not you have bought a long or a short leg. Long leg will still have the rump on it.

Trim all visible skin and fat from the leg of lamb. Take a small sharp knife and insert about 10 to 12 little pockets into the flesh in which you will stuff a clove of garlic and a few fresh rosemary leaves.

Rub with olive oil, season with salt and pepper and cook as for Leg of Lamb Provencale Style (see page 240).

Please see the DVD for further information.

Barbecuing would have to be the ultimate when it comes to entertaining outdoors.

It's not just the theatre of watching the food cook or the aromas wafting around the backyard, it's that a barbie can make even an ordinary cook look good!

It's all in the preparation. A successful barbie relies on a little pre-planning. The average piece of steak or a set of ribs will generally benefit from a good dry rub or a dose of garlic before they hit the grill. And the result is to die for.

Today's barbies are not necessarily your traditional 8 bricks, slab of iron and some old roof tiles or half a 44 gallon drum. The technology that has gone into the modern day barbie is all about making the cook look good.

But at the end of the day, they're still a great gathering point.

So anyhow, throw another shrimp (prawn) on the barbie and get out there and give it a go!

bbqelements

BBQ King Prawns with Sauce Bois Boudran

Serves: 4

In the first month of hosting Fresh, I was fortunate enough to have Michel Roux as a guest chef. Wow, I was in awe! Here was this chef of chefs on my show. He prepared a couple of dishes, the most memorable being the Sauce Bois Boudran. Very simple and absolutely delicious, using basic pantry items with the addition of a few fresh herbs and served over roasted spatchcock. Here's my interpretation of it, served with barbecued prawns.

20 large king prawns
olive oil
salt and freshly ground black pepper

Leave prawn (shrimp) head and tail intact, removing the thin shell from around the flesh, along with the intestinal tract. Crank up the barbecue to a medium high heat if you have one, if not a griddle pan will do just fine.

When the cooking surface is hot, rub prawns with a little olive oil, salt and pepper and place on the hot surface. Cook until golden then turn. Depending on the size, the prawns should only take a couple of minutes on either side. Serve dressed with sauce Bois Boudran.

The Sauce

100ml (3¼ fl oz) olive oil
35ml (1 fl oz) white wine vinegar
Salt and freshly ground pepper
2½ tbs tomato sauce
1 tsp Worcestershire sauce
3 drops Tabasco sauce

100g (3½ oz) eschalot, finely chopped
10g tarragon
5g chervil
5g chives

Combine the oil, vinegar, a pinch of salt and a good grind of pepper in a bowl. Stir with a fork then add tomato sauce, Worcestershire, Tabasco, chopped eschalots and all the snipped* herbs.

Adjust the seasoning with salt and pepper and keep at room temperature: the sauce is ready to use straight away, however will keep for up to 3 days in an airtight container.

*Snipping herbs with a pair of scissors or shears will eliminate some of the bruising that a dull knife will generally cause.

Whole Baked Snapper

I understand not everyone can sit down and appreciate a whole fish, especially one that is looking right back at them. But once you can get over this fear you will understand how much more flavoursome and juicier something is when cooked on the bone.

I highly recommend cranking up your barbecue just for this meal, if you don't have a barbie, a griddle pan will do just fine.

1 whole snapper (500g/1lb), scaled and gutted (see DVD for tips)

50ml (1 ½ fl oz) extra virgin olive oil

3 sprigs fresh thyme

2 eschalots, finely sliced

⅓ bunch flat leaf parsley

1 small bulb of fennel

30ml (1 fl oz) verjuice* (white wine or lemon juice)

Sea salt and freshly ground black pepper

3 small radish

Fresh rocket leaves

1 lemon

Preheat barbecue or griddle pan. Using a sharp knife score both sides of the fish 3 times along the back bone, all the way to the bone. This will cause some moisture loss, but the fish will definitely cook quicker.

Take a piece of foil twice the length of the fish and pour half of the oil in the centre. Place the fish on top.

Stuff the thyme, eschalots, parsley stalks and the fennel tops into the cavity of the fish. Douse fish with remaining olive oil, verjuice and seasonings.

Wrap in foil leaving no openings and place straight onto barbecue. Fish should take around 8–9 minutes on each side. After this time, remove from heat and allow to rest in foil for a further 5 minutes before serving.

Serve with a salad of sliced radish and fennel tossed with rocket leaves, olive oil and a squeeze of fresh lemon juice.

Verjuice is unfermented green grape juice.

BBQ Veal Chop with Basil & Tomatoes

Serves: 1

A man's gotta to have his meat!! I love this because it's one of those meals that is so quick and easy to put together and always tastes delicious.

1 Veal chop (approximately 225g/8 oz)

2 tbs olive oil

Sea salt & freshly ground black pepper

1 clove garlic, bruised

3 basil leaves, torn

1 Roma tomato, sliced

2 bocconcini(baby mozzarella), sliced

Take the veal chop, cover it with a thick piece of plastic and carefully bash it with the smooth side of a meat mallet, or a rolling pin until about 6mm (¼ inch) thick. Brush with a little of the oil, season with salt and pepper and place it straight onto a hot barbecue or griddle plate.

Depending on the thickness of the chop, cook for a few minutes on one side turn and rub with bruised garlic. Discard garlic when finished.

Scatter with basil, tomato and bocconcini (baby mozzaella), finish cooking and place onto a serving plate. Drizzle with good olive oil and scatter with basil leaves.

"The story of barbecue is the story of america: settlers arrive on great unspoiled continent, discover wondrous riches, set them on fire and eat them". VINCE STATEN

Texan BBQ Ribs

It doesn't matter which part of Texas you're in or which restaurant, they all claim to have the best barbecue in the world. If you're a local you call it 'Q' for short. Texas is certainly well known for its big servings of barbecued meats, dry rubbed with herbs and spices before being pit smoked to perfection. For good barbecued ribs there is no way around the 4 to 6 hours of slow cooking, this is how it gains the essential smokey flavour and gelatinous texture.

Here's a recipe for pork spare ribs, using your oven for most of the work, needing only 15 to 20 minutes max on the barbecue, basically to reheat and serve. This recipe consists of two parts; the rub and the sauce with which the ribs will be basted and served. Be prepared for a good day of preparation. Sorry there are no short cuts to good ribs.

Serves: 4 to 6

BBQ sauce

1 cup tomato sauce/ketchup

1 cup tinned crushed tomatoes, pureed

½ cup (110g/3¾ oz) brown sugar

1 tsp Worcestershire sauce

½ tsp Tabasco sauce

1 lemon, zest and juice

60ml (2 fl oz) cider vinegar

1 fresh hot chilli, seeds removed and finely chopped

¼ cup grated onion

To prepare the barbecue sauce, place all ingredients in a saucepan, bring to the boil then lower temperature and slowly simmer and reduce for about 15 to 20 minutes. Season with salt and pepper. This sauce will keep for a good month, provided it's refrigerated. It can certainly be made a day in advance.

Spice Rub

Some speciality shops sell spice rubs for convenience, but if not, here's a recipe.

½ cup (110g/3¾ oz) brown sugar

¼ cup paprika

1 tbs ground black pepper

1½ tbs sea salt

1 tsp cayenne pepper (or ½ tsp for a more mild flavour)

2 tbs grated onion or 1 tbs onion powder

½ tsp chilli flakes

2 American Pork Spare Rib Racks (approx 1.5kg/3⅓ lbs)*

Mix all spice rub ingredients together. Using half of the spice rub, massage into the ribs and let stand for a minimum of 10 minutes.

Preheat oven to 110° to 115°C (230° to 240°F). Sprinkle the rest of the spice rub over the ribs, place on a wire rack and slow roast for 4 to 5 hours.

Bring half of the barbecue sauce to room temperature and baste the ribs after the first 2 hours, every 45 minutes until cooked. Ribs are cooked when a knife can be pushed into the meat between the bones with no resistance. Remove from oven and chill. The ribs are now ready for barbecuing.

Place ribs on the char-grill part of your barbecue. Whether it's a top of the range barbecue or a backyard job, the idea is that what ever you choose to finish the ribs on is hot, so preheating is essential.

Cook for a good 5 to 10 minutes each side. Serve with remaining sauce.

*There are 2 types of ribs. American Pork Spare Ribs are a whole rack of ribs. The other ribs are a cross section.

BBQ Spatchcock

Spatchcock is basically a small chicken, nothing bigger than a 500g (1 lb) which is perfect for the barbecue as it cooks quickly and is a great portion size for one. Like chicken it lends itself to a wide variety of flavours. I love the pure simplicity of fresh basil pushed under the skin and barbecued 'till crisp skinned with moist flesh. I have left the rib cage intact which helps retain moisture, however if you would like to bone out the spatchcock completely, check out the directions on the DVD.

I have served this dish with a wedge of iceberg lettuce dressed with olive oil and lemon juice.

Serves: 2

2 spatchcock
2 basil leaves
2 tbs olive oil
salt and freshly ground black pepper

264

Preheat barbecue for a good 15 minutes before using.

Cut spatchcock down backbone using a sharp knife or a pair of kitchen shears and flatten.

Carefully separate the skin from the breast meat near the neck and push the basil leaves under the skin. Drizzle with olive oil and season well with salt and pepper.

Place onto a preheated barbecue skin side down. Cook for 5 minutes, turn spatchcock and cook for a further 4 minutes or until crisp and cooked through.

For a Portuguese style flavour,

Zest and juice of ½ an orange
2 tbs olive oil
1 clove garlic, finely chopped
2 tsp paprika
½ tsp salt
1 small chilli, seeds removed and finely chopped

Combine the ingredients and rub into spatchcock. Marinate in the refrigerator for a good hour before cooking.

Smokey Corn and Pepper Salsa

Serves: 4

This is a great little snack finished with a handful of fresh crab meat, or served as a bruschetta topping.

2 corn cobs, husks still intact
2 tbs olive oil
Salt and freshly ground black pepper
2 red capsicums (bell peppers)
1 Spanish (red) onion, finely diced
3 tbs extra virgin olive oil
1 lime
½ bunch shredded basil leaves

Preheat a barbecue or grill pan, a good 15 minutes before using.

Pull back the husks of the corn. Remove the silky threads and then replace the leaves. Soak corn in water for 30 minutes. Drain well. Pull back the husks again and brush over oil, salt and pepper. Cook corn with the husk on, turning occasionally, on high heat for 20 to 25 minutes.

Meanwhile, place capsicum on the grill turning frequently until evenly blackened. Remove from heat, place into a bowl and cover with plastic wrap. Set aside for 20 minutes to sweat, this allows the skin to loosen. Peel the capsicum, removing charred skin and seeds. NEVER EVER run under water, as this will wash away their sweetness. When cleaned cut into a small dice.

When corn is cooked, remove blackened husk to reveal the cooked corn kernels. Place the corn on its side on a chopping board, using a sharp knife slice away the cooked corn, discarding the cob.

Mix the peppers and corn together along with the Spanish onion, season with extra virgin olive oil, salt, pepper and a touch of lime juice. Scatter with basil leaves.

Skewers

When it comes to cocktail parties or nibblies, I am rather fond of skewers, for a few reasons, preparation is relatively simple, being prepared in advanced allows more time with guests or family, and being on a stick relieves the need for extra cutlery and having to wash up.

Here's my top 10.

For all of the skewers below soak the skewers in water for 1 hour before threading. For cooking skewers the barbecue or pan must be hot and well oiled to stop sticking.

Serves: 2 skewers per person

Scallops with Roquefort

Thread scallops onto skewers, douse in olive oil, season with salt and pepper and cook for 30 to 40 seconds on both sides. To serve, top with crumbled Roquefort cheese.

Tuna with Lime and Black Pepper

Thread pieces of tuna (around 7cm/ 2¾ inch x 2cm/¾ inch x 1cm/½ inch) onto skewers and marinate in a little lime zest and black pepper for 20 minutes. Season with salt and grill on each side for 30 to 40 seconds, or to your liking. Finish with fresh lime juice.

Squid with Lemon and Chilli

Clean and score squid (information can be found in the DVD accompanying this book). Thread onto skewers then rub with a little lemon zest, fresh chilli, salt and pepper. Grill for 20 to 30 seconds on each side, squeeze over fresh lime juice and serve.

Prawn with Szechuan Pepper

Peel prawns, leaving the tail piece on and thread onto skewers. Rub with salt and Szechuan pepper (if not available, cracked pepper or five spice powder can be used) and grill for 30 seconds each side. Serve with a squeeze of fresh lime juice (optional).

Haloumi with Rosemary

Carefully thread pieces of Haloumi cheese (around 7cm/2¾ inch x 2cm/¾ inch x 1cm/½ inch) onto a skewer. Marinate with fresh rosemary and a small amount of olive oil. Place onto a grill and cook until golden on each side, around 30 seconds.

Turkish Kofte with Minted Yoghurt

Mix 250g/9 oz ground/minced beef with 1 tablespoon of finely chopped onion, 1 tablespoon of chopped parsley, a good pinch of salt, ½ tsp of ground cumin and ½ tsp hot smoked paprika.

Tomato, Mushroom and Zucchini

Thread a cherry tomato, a button mushroom and a piece of zucchini onto a skewer remembering all need to be of the same thickness. Season with salt and pepper and grill until lightly browned/charred, approximately 30 to 40 seconds.

Chicken with 5 spice

Thread thin strips of chicken breast on skewers. Once chicken is threaded, twist the chicken around the skewer. Season with salt and 5 spice powder and cook on grill until golden, approximately 1 minute each side.

Chilli Beef Sticks

Thread thin strips of rump steak (7cm/2¾ inch x 2cm/¾ inch x ½ cm/¼ inch) onto a skewer and season with a mixture of 1 tsp paprika, 1 tsp mixed herbs, ½ tsp salt and ½ tsp ground pepper. Place on hot grill and cook for approximately 20 to 30 seconds on each side.

Chorizo and Chicken Liver

Cut a Chorizo sausage into 1cm slices. Thread onto a skewer along with a chicken liver (sinew removed) and another piece of Chorizo. Grill for 40 to 50 seconds on each side.

Place all ingredients in a bowl and mix thoroughly. Using wet hands, mould mixture around a skewer, making a "sausage" shape, making around 10 skewers. Lay Kofte on grill/flatplate and cook until golden on each side, approximately 1 minute each side. Serve with minted yoghurt.

Minted Yoghurt:
100g/3½ oz plain (unsweetened) yoghurt, 1 tbs olive oil, 2 tbs finely shredded mint leaves, 1 tbs lemon juice and a pinch of salt and pepper.

Plank Elements

Here's a great addition to your next barbecue, a plank, used for Plank Cooking, first discovered by the Pacific Northwest Indians in America. They cooked their salmon on a damp cedar plank and found it enhanced the flavour of the fresh fish.

Plank cooking relies on the trapping of smoke under the hood of your barbecue and allows food to keep its moisture, whilst also taking on a fantastic light, smokey flavour. Plank cooking is recommended only for those who have a barbecue with a hood.

First things first, you need to get a cooking plank. You have to be really careful when choosing a wood to use for plank cooking, you must REALLY make sure that the wood has not been treated with any chemicals at all. If there are chemicals in the wood, then they can be toxic.

For more info on woods that are good for plank cooking, or to buy some planks already cut, go to my website www.manicj.com and yes, that was a direct plug. But you'll also find a lot more info on plank cooking there too, so it's worth a read.

Here are 6 of my favourite plank cooking recipes, but first some basics…

Basics for All Plank Recipes

1. Soak your planks in water for a minimum of 6 hours. As planks have a tendancy to float, be sure to weight them down.

2. Pre heat your barbecue to 250 to 260°C with the hood closed.

3. Remove planks from water when ready for use and place them on the hot barbecue grill plates. Allow the planks to smoulder for around 5 to 7 minutes. When you turn planks over you should have a blackened surface and the wood smell should be prominent.

4. If for some reason your plank is not soaked for the correct amount of time, not weighted down or your barbecue is too hot, you may have a small flame come from the plank. In this case, put the flame out with a little water, we recommend a small spritzer bottle.

5. Your plank is now ready for cooking!

Planks

Plank Salmon

Take 1 piece of salmon (around 180 to 200gm/7oz), skin intact and bones removed and rub with 1 tablespoon (20ml/½ fl oz) olive oil and season with salt and pepper.

Place flesh side down onto a charred plank surface and cook for 6 to 8 minutes on the barbecue (depending on thickness) and remove. To check if your salmon is cooked, press the flesh with your index finger, if the flesh springs back, your fish is ready.

Planked Whole Trout

Take 1 whole trout of around 300 to 400gm (10½ to 14oz). Place 6 sprigs of fresh thyme into its cavity, along with a liberal seasoning of salt and pepper. Rub the skin of the fish with olive oil and season with salt and pepper.

Place fish onto a charred plank surface and cook for 8 to 10 minutes on the barbecue (depending on thickness) and remove. To check if your trout is cooked, press the thicker part of the flesh with your index finger, if the flesh springs back, your fish is ready.

Planked Figs with Proscuitto and Gorgonzola

Take 3 fresh figs and wrap each fig in a thin slice of proscuitto, pancetta or bacon. With a small knife make a cross (x) on the top of the fig and insert a small piece or gorgonzola* cheese (optional).

Set figs on a charred plank surface and cook for 4 to 6 minutes on the barbecue and remove. When your figs are ready, the proscuitto will have shrunk, the cheese melted and there will be juice seeping from the figs. Allow figs 2 to 3 minutes to cool.

*Roquefort or mozzarella cheese may be substituted.

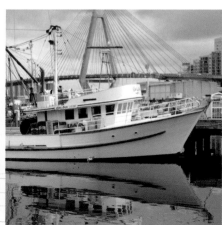

Planked Lamb Rump with Walnut Oil and Garlic

Take 1 lamb rump of around 220 to 250gm (7¾ to 9oz) and rub with 1 tablespoon (20ml/½ fl oz) of walnut oil (extra virgin olive oil could also be used), 1 clove of sliced garlic and a heavy grinding of black pepper and allow to marinate for 2 hours, preferably overnight.

Place lamb rump onto a charred plank surface and cook for 15 to 20 minutes on the barbecue (depending on thickness) and remove. To check if your lamb is cooked, press the thicker part of the flesh with your index finger, if the flesh springs back, your lamb is ready. Then allow for an extra 5 to 10 minutes for the lamb to rest – the juices of the meat will settle and the smokiness intensify.

Planked Kingfish

Take 1 piece of kingfish (around 180 to 200gm/7oz) or other white fleshed fish, skin intact and bones removed and rub with 1 tablespoon (20ml/½ fl oz) olive oil and season with salt and pepper.

Place flesh side down onto a charred plank surface and cook for 6 to 8 minutes on the barbecue (depending on thickness) and remove. To check if your kingfish is cooked, press the flesh with your index finger, if the flesh springs back, your fish is ready.

Planked Whole Chicken with Lime and Chilli Butter

Take 1 whole chicken of around 1.0 to 1.2kg (2¼ to 2½lb) and remove from it's wrapping and pat dry with paper/kitchen towel and set aside.

In a bowl, mix together 100gm (3½oz) softened butter, 1 small hot chilli – finely chopped, the juice and zest of 1 lime (lemon could be substituted), pinch of salt and freshly ground black pepper and mix evenly.

Take the chicken and with your index finger, make a "pocket" between the skin and the flesh of the chicken breast, through the neck cavity. Stuff the butter mixture into the pocket and spread evenly.

Place the chicken onto a charred plank surface breast side up and cook for 45 to 50 minutes on the barbecue and remove. To check if your chicken is cooked, place a knife in between the thigh and the breast. If the juices run out clear, your chicken is cooked. Then allow for an extra 5 to 10 minutes for the chicken to rest – the juices of the chicken will settle and the smokiness intensify.

279

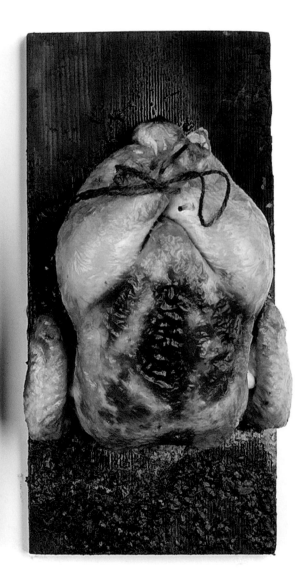

I find it so funny sitting at a restaurant with a few friends after main course has been cleared and the dessert menu hits the table. Everyone looks around for a little encouragement in the hope that if someone else orders, it'll be OK for you to order too. Your guilty conscience will have been suppressed by another's need for a sweet ending to the meal. You'll feel validated.

Fact is, I don't know too many people who don't like dessert, whether it's the simplicity of a poached pear or the extravagance of a double baked chocolate and cognac soufflé. But the trick is portion control.

I like to indulge in something sweet and rich every now and then, but I just make sure I don't over do it. So my sweet elements are not so much about stripping away the fat and sugars (well maybe some are), they're more about not having too much of a good thing. Some are quick and easy, others a little more complex. All divine, though!

Anzac Biscuits

Makes approximately 16

Here's a little taste of Australian pride, the humble Anzac biscuit.

Basic pantry cooking at its best. If golden syrup is not available, substitute with honey, will be slightly sweeter in flavour though.

This is a great one for the kids to help with.

1 cup (160g/5 ½ oz) wholemeal plain flour
1 cup (90g/3 oz) rolled oats
1 cup (90g/3 oz) desiccated coconut
¾ cup (170g/6 oz) brown sugar
125g (4½ oz) butter
2 tbs golden syrup*
1 tsp bicarbonate soda/baking soda

285

Note: In America a biscuit is what we in Australia would call a scone, so this is an American equivalent of a cookie.

Preheat oven to 170°C (340°F). Line a baking tray with parchment paper. Mix flour, oats, coconut and sugar together.

Melt the butter and golden syrup together in a small saucepan over a low heat. Combine the bicarbonate soda with 2 tbs of water in a small bowl. Mix into the melted butter mixture and immediately pour into the dry ingredients and mix well to form a dough.

Take spoonfuls of the mixture and roll into balls. Place on baking tray and flatten to 1cm (⅖th inch) thick. Bake for about 12 to 15 minutes or until golden, allow biscuits to cool before serving.

Bittersweet Chocolate & Calvados Truffles

These are rich but not quite as sweet as a milk chocolate truffle. The bittersweet chocolate and crème fraiche together give a very sophisticated taste. If crème fraiche is not available, substitute sour cream. A little more time and patience is needed when coating these truffles, but it's well worth the effort. This recipe does make a large amount of truffles, feel free to halve the recipe for a smaller quantity.

Serves: 60 pieces

200g (7 oz) crème fraiche
100g (3½ oz) thickened/heavy cream
80g (2¾ oz) glucose
500g (1.1lb) bitter sweet chocolate (61 to 66% cocoa mass), chopped
130g (4½ oz) butter
60ml (2 fl oz) Calvados

For coating
250g (8¾ oz) bittersweet chocolate
Gold leaf* (optional – can be found at speciality art shops and cooking stores)
OR
100g (3½ oz) dark unsweetened cocoa

Over a moderate heat, bring the crème fraiche, cream and glucose almost to boiling point then remove from the heat.

Gently pour the hot liquid over the chopped chocolate and butter, stirring with a spatula until smooth. Cool slightly then stir in Calvados.

Allow the chocolate mixture to firm up and set in the refrigerator for 30 to 40 minutes.

Once set and quite firm, pipe mixture into little tear drops onto a chilled tray lined with parchment paper or foil, I find a size 8 plain nozzle for piping the chocolate works best. Alternatively take a warm teaspoon and pull through the chocolate to give you small pieces, chill again for another hour.

Meanwhile, melt 250g (8¾ oz) of chocolate in a bowl set over a larger bowl of warm water, no hotter than 60°C (140°F), until chocolate has melted.

Remove truffle mixture from refrigerator, and using clean hands, roll into balls. Drop each truffle into the melted chocolate and roll around using a fork until completely coated. Remove, draining excess chocolate, prior to setting on parchment paper.

Keep refrigerated until 10 minutes before serving. Prior to serving, place a small piece of gold leaf on top of each truffle using a small amount of oil to adhere.

*Gold leaf is edible.

Note: Alternatively, truffles can be removed from the refrigerator and rolled in cocoa (as for milk chocolate truffles on page 309).

Buttermilk Pudding

Serves: 2

This is an impressive, no fuss summer dessert that can be made in advance and plated just before serving.

3 tsp powdered gelatine OR 7g (¼ oz) leaf gelatine
⅓ cup (80ml/2½ fl oz) cream
¾ cup (170g/6 oz) sugar
½ vanilla bean split, seeds removed and reserved
600ml (1 pint) buttermilk
½ cup (125ml/4 fl oz) thickened/heavy cream (whipped to semi-soft peaks)
2 punnets strawberries
2 tbs icing sugar
1 lime

Note: The moulds I have used in this recipe are of around ¾ cup capacity (180/5¾ fl oz).

If using powdered gelatine, soak in 2 tbs of warm water. For leaf gelatine, soak in 200mls (6½ fl oz) of cool water until softened, remembering to squeeze out excess water before using.

Heat cream, sugar, vanilla bean and seeds together until sugar has dissolved. Stir in dissolved gelatine. Allow to cool, stirring from time to time.

Stir in buttermilk and cool slightly. Fold ½ cup of whipped cream into the buttermilk base and fill the moulds*. Chill for at least 4 hours before serving.

Take 1 punnet of the strawberries, removing the green stalks, and puree with icing sugar and a squeeze of lime juice, until smooth.

To serve, dip the moulds into hot water and using a small knife, release the pudding by tilting the mould and levering the knife down the side of the cream. Invert onto plate and serve with pureed strawberries and remaining fresh strawberries.

Caramelised Gingerbread with Glazed Apples and Mascarpone

This recipe reminds me of times when the pastry chef at Bistro Moncur would make gingerbread. I don't quite remember the dessert as such but the off cuts that she would trim off for the staff to eat I will never forget, definitely the best part. This recipe reflects those crusty trimmings along with apples, which seem to be in season all year round and the mascarpone cream is just pure indulgence.

Serves: Loaf will serve 12 slices. Apples 4 portions.

The Gingerbread

200g (7oz) soft butter

250g (8¾ oz) brown sugar

400g (14 oz) plain flour

3 tsp ground ginger

2 tsp cinnamon

2 tsp bicarbonate of soda

1 cup (250ml/8 fl oz) boiling water

1 cup (350g/¾ lb) golden syrup or honey

2 eggs

*For a non alcoholic version of this recipe, substitute the brandy for a fruit juice such as orange or apple.

**If this happens and providing only 60ml has been added, when the alcohol burns off the flame will subside. Do not panic, but be cautious.

Preheat oven to 175°C (350°F). Line 2 small loaf tins with greaseproof or parchment paper. Beat butter and sugar in a food processor until creamy. Add eggs, one at a time to form a smooth batter. In a separate bowl sift dry ingredients together. Mix boiling water and syrup together. Fold into batter, in batches, alternating with dry ingredients. Divide between loaf tins. Bake for approximately 45 minutes, or until firm to the touch or deep golden in colour.

The Apples

4 ripe apples (I quite often will use Golden Delicious)

2 tbs butter

¼ cup (60g/ 2 oz) sugar

1 bay leaf (fresh if possible)

60ml (2 fl oz) brandy*

120g mascarpone

¼ tsp vanilla extract

Peel the apples, removing the core, and cut into eighths. In a heavy based frying pan, melt butter and sugar together, add apples and bay leaf and cook until golden, tossing from time to time. When evenly coloured, remove from heat, pour in brandy and return to the heat, being aware that the alcohol may ignite.**

Beat mascarpone with vanilla and a little of the apple syrup from the pan, just enough to sweeten, not too much. Keep chilled.

To Serve

Take the cooled loaf of gingerbread and cut into 2cm (¾ inch) thick slices.

Butter both sides of the gingerbread, then dust with a thin coating of caster sugar.

Place into a pre-heated pan (not too hot) and cook until sugar caramelises, turn and repeat on other side.

Place on plate and top with warm glazed apples and a generous scoop of the mascarpone cream.

The gingerbread is the only part of this dish suitable for freezing, if it makes it that far. It's really nice the next day with salted butter.

For Something Different

Crumble gingerbread into softened vanilla ice cream, mix well and allow to freeze for approximately 2 to 3 hours. To serve, scoop into glasses topped with fresh cream.

Damien's Chocolate and Cognac Soufflé

Serves: 8

Note: There really is no substiture for the alcohol content in this recipe as it provides the balance and complexity of flavour.

This is the double baked soufflé that featured in the dinner party section of my DVD. It is a wonderful dish to make ahead of time and always looks impressive when served. This is one for the adults and cognac could be replaced with brandy.

30g (1 oz) soft butter

2 tbs plain flour

2 tbs sugar

240ml (8½ fl oz) milk

40g (1½ oz) cocoa

120g (4¼ oz) sugar

4 egg yolks, well beaten

30g (1 oz) custard powder

60ml (2 fl oz) Cognac

6 egg whites

2 tbs sugar, extra

160g (5½ oz) bittersweet chocolate, finely chopped

Coffee Cream

2 tsp instant coffee

2 tsp Cognac

600ml (1 pint) cream

1 tsp vanilla extract

Preheat oven to 175°C (350°F). Prepare 8 soufflé moulds of around ¾ cup (180ml/5¾ fl oz) capacity by brushing with soft butter and dusting lightly with the combined flour and sugar mixture.

Heat milk with cocoa and half of the sugar. In a bowl, whisk egg yolks, custard powder and the remaining sugar together. Whisk in hot milk. Return to the pan and bring to the boil. Whisk continuously, over medium heat until mixture thickens (approximately 5 to 6 minutes). Allow to cool slightly before whisking in the Cognac.

In a large clean bowl, (preferably copper) whisk egg whites until soft peaks form, then slowly incorporate the extra sugar whilst whisking until dissolved. Egg whites should be quite firm. Fold the egg whites and chopped chocolate into the cocoa mixture, a third at a time, carefully folding after each batch is added. Ladle into prepared moulds until ¾ full.

Preheat oven to 175°C (350°F). Place the soufflés into a deep baking dish filled with 4cm (1½ inch) of boiling water. Bake for approximately 20 to 25 minutes. The puddings should have risen a good few centimetres above the rim of the mould. Remove from oven and allow to cool slightly leaving in the water bath.

To prepare Coffee Cream; dissolve instant coffee in extra Cognac, then combine with cream and vanilla. When ready to serve, turn soufflés out into a gratin dish. Cover with coffee cream and bake in a preheated oven at 200°C (400°F) for 8 to 10 minutes until risen. Serve with fresh cream.

Creamy Rice Pudding with Cherries in Sparkling Burgundy

The picture says it all! I love the texture and flavour of a sweet rice pudding; remember portion control, and no double dipping!

Serves: 6

P.S. The cherries are amazing, but don't feel obligated to poach them if you're in a hurry. If you have good cherries serve them fresh.

500ml (16 fl oz) milk

1 vanilla bean, split lengthways and seeds scraped with the back of a knife

100g (3.5 oz) arborio rice

250ml (8 fl oz) thickened/heavy cream

50g (1¾ oz) sugar

Zest of a lemon

Pinch of Salt

200mls (6½ fl oz) cream, lightly whipped

Bring milk, vanilla seeds and bean pod to the boil. Stir in the rice and thickened cream, lower the temperature, stirring occasionally, for 20 minutes or until rice is tender.

Add the sugar, lemon zest and salt. Transfer to a bowl and allow to cool. Just before serving, fold through lightly whipped cream.

The Cherries

750ml (1⅓ pints) sparkling burgundy (sparkling red wine)

500g (1.1lb) sugar

1 cinnamon quill

500g (1.1lb) cherries, stems trimmed

2 limes

Note: The cherries will keep for up to a month providing they are well refrigerated.

In a stainless steel pan, pour in the burgundy, add sugar and stir until dissolved. Add cinnamon and cherries. Cover with a piece of greaseproof paper ensuring the cherries are submerged.

Place pan over a low heat and bring to the boil. Once boiling, remove from heat and leave cherries to cool in liquid. When cool, strain liquid into another pan, return to a high heat and simmer until reduced by half and syrupy.

Add enough lime juice to balance the sweetness then pour syrup back over the cherries and chill well before serving. Serve with creamy rice pudding and filigree wafer (see page 297).

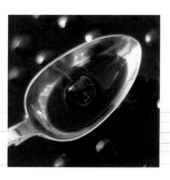

Filigree Wafer

Serves: 4 to 5

This little number is the icing on the cake, the WOW factor when trying to impress; it looks pretty special served alongside even the simplest of desserts. The raw mixture keeps well, frozen for up to a month.*

55g (2 oz) of egg white
65g (2¼ oz) icing sugar, sifted
55g (2 oz) plain flour

Note: The cooked filigree will keep well in an airtight container for up to 3 days.

Whisk together egg white and icing sugar. Add plain flour and mix well. If you have time, allow to rest for a good hour.

Preheat oven to 160°C (320°F). Prepare a small piping bag from parchment paper, with the finest of tips to allow a fine stream of the paste to flow through when lightly squeezed.

Half fill the piping bag and fold over the top. Have a baking tray lined with parchment paper ready to pipe the paste onto. There are no set rules for shapes you want to create; I find a simple free form lattice pattern always looks special, keeping it at about the size of your hand.

If you want to make a conical shape, after removing from the oven, lay wafer and parchment paper over a rolling pin. When cool, remove from rolling pin and carefully separate from paper.

*To defrost mixture remove from freezer an hour before using.

297

"cooking is like love, it should be entered into with abandon or not at all". harriet van horne

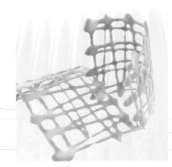

Chocolate and Vanilla Snaps

Here's a simple cookie that's light, crisp and even better tastes great. Make a double batch if you feel up to it, the dough freezes perfectly well for up to 2 months. Makes about 20 to 25 cookies.

Serves: 20 to 25

125g (4½ oz) butter

125g (4½ oz) sugar

1 tbs vanilla extract

1 egg*

1 tbs white or dark rum, optional

250g (8¾ oz) plain flour

¼ tsp baking powder/baking soda

2 tbs cocoa

1 egg white, lightly beaten

298

Beat the butter, sugar and vanilla until light and creamy in texture. Add egg and rum and beat well.

Sift the flour and baking powder over the butter mixture and beat quickly until combined. Divide the mixture in half and add cocoa to one half to colour. Wrap each piece individually and refrigerate until firm (approximately 30 minutes).

When firm, roll out both portions of dough to make a rectangle about 5mm (⅛th inch) thick and of similar size. Brush the plain dough with egg white; place the chocolate dough on top. Brush with egg white and roll up like a pinwheel, starting with the longer side of the rectangle. Chill for 1 hour.

Preheat oven to 170°C (340°F). When dough is firm, cut thin slices and lay on baking trays. Bake for about 10 minutes. Leave on trays for 5 minutes then transfer to a wire rack to cool and firm.

TIP: For marbled cookies, cut thick slices from the pinwheel dough, turn onto a lightly floured bench and roll to a thickness of about 3mm. Using a cutter, cut desired shapes and bake as above.

Note: Always break eggs into a separate bowl before adding to any mixture to ensure you don': add a bad egg.

Fresh Fig and Hazelnut Tart

Serves: 2

Note: This dish lends itself to a variety of fruits such as peaches or plums.

50g (1¾ oz) unsalted butter, softened
¼ cup (60g/2 oz) caster sugar
1 egg
¼ cup (25g/¾ oz) ground hazelnuts/hazelnut meal
1 tbs plain flour
Pinch of salt
1 sheet frozen butter puff pastry, thawed
1 egg yolk (lightly beaten)
3 fresh figs
Icing sugar, for dusting

Pre-heat oven to 240°C (465°F).

Beat the butter and sugar together until pale in colour. Whisk in the egg until well combined.

Gently fold in the ground hazelnut, flour and salt, being careful not to over work the flour. Set aside and rest 15 minutes before using.

Take the sheet of puff pastry, and with a sharp knife trim the edges. This will allow the pastry to rise evenly. Cut the pastry into even quarters, take the knife and cut a 1½cm border around 2 pieces of the pastry leaving you with just the frames. Brush the remaining 2 pieces of pastry lightly with egg yolk, placing the frames on top. This allows for a thick crust. Take a fork and pierce the centre of both pieces of pastry.

Spread the centre of each pastry with a ½cm of the hazelnut cream. Split the figs and arrange over the cream, Dust with icing sugar. Bake in the oven for 12 to 15 minutes or until pastry is risen and golden and the figs are glazed. Best served with a helping of vanilla ice cream.

Fresh Fruit Sticks with Lime and Chilli Syrup

Someone once said, the simple things in life are often the best. Some of my favourite meals in Asia have always ended with simple pieces of fresh seasonal fruit, either plain or with a syrup like the one I have listed in this recipe.

The key to finished fruit sticks that are "perfection" requires a little extra time and precise cutting and, unfortunately, a degree of wastage. The result is a feast for both the eyes and the palate.

Feel free to adopt a rustic approach to your fruit sticks, thus having less wastage.

Some seasonal suggestions would be: watermelon, pineapple, honeydew, rockmelon (cantaloupe), strawberries, peaches and mangoes. Generally any fruit that can maintain it's shape after being placed on a skewer is suitable.

Serves: 6

Lime & Chilli Syrup

Bamboo skewers

⅓ cup (70g/4 ½ oz) sugar

⅓ cup (80ml/2 ½ fl oz) water

½ birds-eye chilli, seeds removed and finely chopped

Bring to the boil, sugar, water, chilli and lime. Simmer for 2 minutes, remove from heat and allow to cool.

To serve brush each stick with lime and chilli syrup, serving immediately.

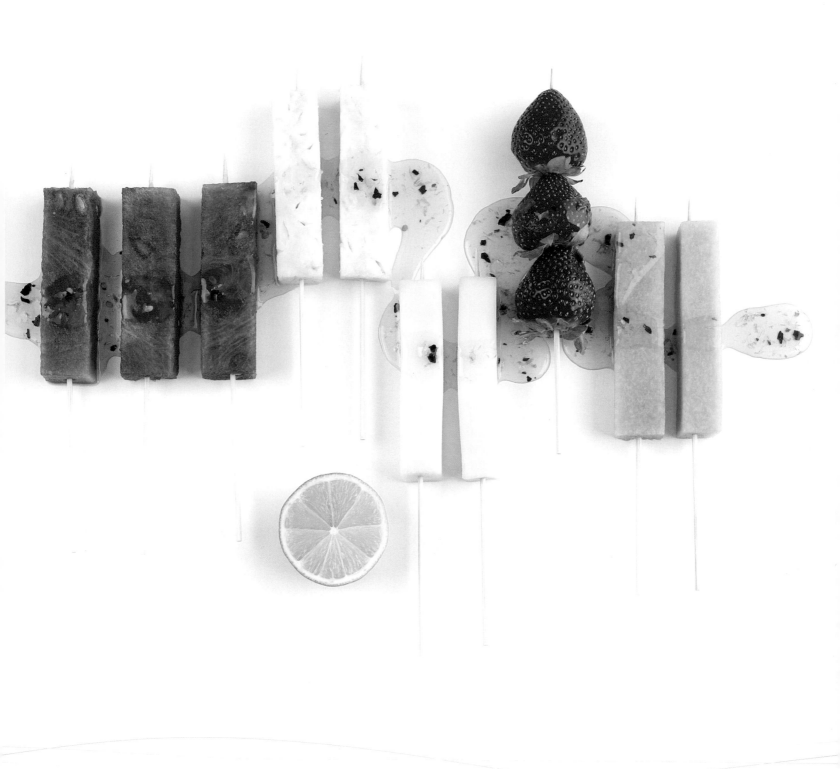

Lavender Blancmange

I love the flavour of lavender, even though it still has an early 1980's appeal. Lavender always works well with almonds.

2½ tsp powdered gelatine or 6g (¼ oz) leaf gelatine

70g (2½ oz) honey

50g (1¾ oz) sugar

250g (8¾ oz) blanched almonds

200ml (6½ fl oz) milk

450ml (14½ fl oz) thickened/heavy cream

2 tsp dried lavender*

Soak the gelatine in 200ml (6½ fl oz) of cold water for 2 to 3 minutes or until softened. Remove and squeeze out excess water. See page 289 for when using powdered gelatine.

Dissolve the honey and sugar in 150ml (4¾ fl oz) of water over a low heat. Don't boil. Add the gelatine and stir to dissolve. Strain through a sieve, set aside and allow to cool.

Place the almonds and lavender in a blender with the milk and 100ml (3¼ fl oz) of water, process to a fine paste. Transfer to a large, double thickness of muslin cloth and squeeze over a bowl to collect the almond milk. This should yield around 250ml (8 fl oz) but if less, top up with milk to make up to 250ml (8 fl oz). Add this to the gelatine syrup, stirring frequently until cooled. Discard almond meal.

Whip the cream to soft peaks and stir a quarter of this into the base almond mixture. Fold through the remaining whipped cream thoroughly. Transfer to 125ml (4 fl oz) moulds or a large glass bowl. Chill for 2 to 3 hours before serving.

To remove from mould, dip into hot water for 5 seconds, slip a small knife down the side of the blancmange to release the vacuum and turn out onto a plate, or if serving from a bowl, scoop blancmange on to a plate using a large kitchen spoon. Serve with fresh fruit such as figs, fresh raspberries or strawberries.

*Lavender for cooking is available in the spice section of your market or from specialist spice stores. If unavailable substitute for another flavour such as vanilla essence (1 tsp) or leave it out.

Nanna's Lemon and Honey Tea

Got to love your Nanna, she always has the remedies for curing a cough or sore throat, whether it was just a spoonful of honey, Vicks™ ointment on the chest or a pot of delicious lemon and honey tea, sometimes with the addition of a few slices of ginger.

It was always a cure, thanks Nanna.

1 whole lemon, cut into 8 wedges
¼ cup honey preferably Manuka honey
from New Zealand if available

Place lemon into a tea pot of some description. Squeeze 4 of the 8 segments into the pot and leave the other 4 segments whole and place in the pot also. Pour over boiling water and let steep for a couple of minutes. Pour tea as required, sweeten with honey.

"my doctor told me to stop having intimate dinners for four, unless there are three other people". orson welles

Pistachio and Saffron Biscotti

I love the crisp texture of freshly baked biscotti. It lends itself to a wide variety of flavours and textures. One of my favourites is pistachio and saffron. Other favourites are almond and star anise or hazelnut and rosemary.

Makes approximately 20 to 30 pieces

Note: 350g (12 oz) of pistachio nuts in the shell should yield 200g (7 oz) of nuts.

2 eggs

1 egg yolk

¾ cup (175g/6 oz) sugar

2 ½ cups (315g/11 oz) plain flour

1 tsp baking powder

200g (7 oz) pistachio nuts

1 large pinch of saffron* steeped in 2 tbs of milk

Beat the whole eggs, egg yolk and sugar with electric beaters until light. Add the dry ingredients and saffron milk and fold through mixture gently to make a dough. Refrigerate for an hour.

Mould the dough into a log shape then roll on a floured bench to form a perfect cylinder.

Preheat oven to 160°C (320°F). Lay the rolled dough onto a greased baking tray and place into the oven for 45 minutes and until golden.

Remove from the oven and allow to cool. When cool, slice at about a 3 mm (⅛ inch) thickness and arrange on the baking tray. Return to the oven and bake for about 25 minutes at 140°C (285°F). Remove and cool on wire racks. Store in an airtight container.

*Adding the saffron to the milk allows for the release of flavour and colour before using.

Poire Belle-Helene; Pears with Chocolate Sauce

Serves: 6

Pears are basically in season all year, with only the fluctuation of price and quality to tell us different. They are definitely at their best come autumn (fall). With several varieties to choose from – William, Beurre Bosc and Packham being the most common, then you have your Corella, Doyenne Du Comice, cocktail etc.

One of the most indulgent ways to eat a pear is to poach it, cover in warm chocolate sauce and scatter it with butter toasted almonds, or crystallised violets. Its name is Poire Belle-Helene and is a classic French dish which achieved its name after the famous operetta by Offenbach.

The Pears

1 litre (1¾ pints) cold water

750g (1¾ lb) sugar

1 lemon, juice and zest

1 vanilla bean, split lengthways and seeds scraped and reserved

6 medium-sized pears (William, if possible)

In a pot that is big enough to hold all of the above ingredients, place everything except the pears. Stir till sugar has almost dissolved. Peel the pears, leave whole and place into the liquid. Cover with a piece of parchment paper to eliminate any moisture loss. Place over heat and bring to the boil.

Once pears have reached boiling point, remove from heat and allow to cool in the same pot. Do not refrigerate, this could affect their sensuous texture. Once cooled to room temperature you may refrigerate for later use for up to 5 days.

The Chocolate Sauce

70g (2½ oz) caster sugar

½ cup (50g/1¾ oz) unsweetened cocoa

175ml (5½ fl oz) warm water

15g (½ oz) butter

Place the sugar, cocoa and water in a thick based saucepan and whisk until combined. Bring to the boil over a gentle heat, reduce temperature to a simmer and continue to cook for a further 2 minutes.
Whisk in the butter, a little at a time, and cook for another minute. Keep the sauce warm until ready to serve.

The Almonds

50g (1¾ oz) butter

3 tbs flaked almonds

Heat the butter in a small frying pan till foaming. Add the almonds and gently toss through the butter till golden, strain off the butter.
To serve, place a scoop of your favourite vanilla ice cream into shallow bowl.
Along side it a poached pear, covered with warm chocolate sauce and a scatter of butter toasted almonds, or crystallised violets if available.

Date and Sour Cream Scones

Makes 6

I love eating scones as a special treat, topped with jam and lashings of cream. The idea with the dates is to add them as a form of fibre. They are chewy and delicious and with the sour cream give an amazing depth of character. Great in the school lunch box or as an after school treat.

250g (8¾ oz) self raising flour

1 tsp baking powder (baking soda)

½ tsp allspice

Pinch of salt

20g (¾ oz) butter

150g (5¼ oz) dates, stone removed and chopped

¼ cup (60g/2 oz) sugar

6 tbs sour cream

80ml (2½ fl oz) water

Preheat oven to 200°C (400°F) and line a baking tray with either a layer of parchment paper or a thin slathering of flour.

Sift flour, baking powder, allspice and salt onto a clean bench; using fingertips rub in butter and make a well in the centre.

Add the dates, sugar and sour cream. Using a plastic scraper or a blunt knife cut the sour cream into the flour, this stops the gluten from being over worked.

When almost mixed to a dough, use your hands to push together, kneading lightly to form a thickish rectangle. Cut into 6 squares.

Place onto baking tray and bake for 10 to 15 minutes. After 10 minutes lower heat to 180°C (350°F) and continue to cook until golden, approximately 5 minutes more.

Pumpkin Scones

Makes 6

Pumpkin scones are called biscuits in the United States. They are synonymous with the Australian state of Queensland, which is home to one of Australia's most popular pumpkins – the Queensland Blue.

Although a Queensland Blue is great for this recipe, any type of pumpkin can be substituted.

250g (8¾ oz) pumpkin, skin and seeds removed, cut into small pieces

2 cups (250g/8¾ oz) self raising flour

1 tsp baking powder

¼ tsp ground nutmeg

Pinch of salt

30g (1 oz) butter

1 egg, lightly beaten

60ml (2 fl oz) milk

Steam pumpkin until tender then place into a dry pan over a moderate heat to cook out any excess moisture. Remove from heat and puree.

Preheat oven to 200°C (400°F) and line a baking tray with either a layer of parchment paper or a thin slathering of flour.

Sift dry ingredients onto a clean bench; using fingertips rub butter into flour and make a well in the centre. Add the pumpkin, egg and milk, using a plastic scraper or a blunt knife cut the wet ingredients into the flour.

When almost mixed to a dough, use your hands to push dough together, kneading lightly to push into a thickish rectangle, cut into 6 squares.

Place onto baking tray and bake for 10 to 15 minutes or until cooked through with a golden blush.

Traditional Scones

Makes 6

The idea with sifting the flour twice is to help lighten the mixture; scones should be light and airy with a golden blush.

250g (8¾ oz) self raising flour
1 tsp baking powder
½ tsp salt
50g (1¾ oz) chilled butter, finely diced
1 cup (250ml/ 8 fl oz) warm milk

Preheat oven to 200°C (400°F). Sift flour, baking powder and salt together, twice. Line a baking tray with either a layer of parchment paper or a thin slathering of flour.

Using fingertips, rub the butter into the flour until it looks 'breadcrumby'. Create a well in the centre of the flour and pour in the milk. Using a stock standard dinner knife, stir the milk into the flour, till just combined. Press mixture together, being careful not to overwork the dough.

Place onto a lightly floured board and cut into 6 little squares.

Bake for 10 to 15 minutes or until golden. I love to serve with a little fresh cream and strawberry jam.

Sticky Date Pudding with Butterscotch Sauce

Makes 4

It certainly is sticky and loaded with dates. This is the ultimate in rich desserts.

20g softened butter

3 tbs caster sugar

100g dates, stones removed

150ml (4¾ fl oz) water

½ tsp bicarbonate soda/baking soda

30g (1 oz) butter

60g (2 oz) sugar

1 egg

100g (3½ oz) self raising flour

1 quantity of butterscotch sauce

Whipped cream for serving

Preheat oven to 200°C (400°F). Using a pastry brush, brush the inside of 4 x 200ml (6½ fl oz) dariole moulds or ramekins with softened butter to coat well. Sprinkle in the sugar, turn the moulds around in your hands so the sugar evenly coats the buttered surface.

Place dates and water into a saucepan and bring to the boil, add the bicarbonate soda and leave to cool. Be aware as it will bubble up. Pour into a blender and puree.

323

Beat the butter and sugar together until creamy; add egg and beat till well incorporated. Add pureed dates to the creamed mixture, and mix well, sift in flour, and gently fold through the mixture.

Pour mixture into prepared moulds to ¾'s full and sit moulds in a baking dish filled with 3.5cm (1½ inches) of boiling water. Bake for 15 to 20 minutes until well risen and when tested with a skewer, it pulls out clean.

Turn out puddings while hot and serve with butterscotch sauce and whipped cream.

Serves 4

Butterscotch Sauce

This sauce is ridiculously decadent, best served over a freshly steamed sticky date pudding.

50g (1¾ oz) butter

70g (2½ oz) brown sugar

100ml (3¼ fl oz) cream

½ tsp vanilla extract

Place all ingredients into a small pan. Bring to the boil, stirring until smooth, simmer for 5 minutes. Refrigerate for 10 minutes before serving.

The Aussie Pavlova

The Pavlova dessert has a meringue base and fresh cream and fruit topping. It is a refreshing summertime favourite. Both Australia and New Zealand claim the pavlova as a national dish. Stories abound as to the history of its creation. They do agree, however, that the dish was named after the famous Russian ballet dancer Anna Pavlova. I have kept this dish simple, just with the addition of passionfruit and blackberries.

Makes 6 small

4 egg whites (120ml/4 fl oz)

¼ tsp cream of tartar

Pinch of salt

½ tsp white vinegar

1 cup (220g/7¾ oz) sugar

1 tsp cornflour

3 drops vanilla extract

1 cup (250ml/8 fl oz) whipped cream

6 passionfruit

1 punnet of blackberries or strawberries

Preheat oven to 120°C / 250°F. Line baking tray with aluminum foil or baking paper.

On a medium speed in an electric mixer or with a hand mixer, beat egg whites with cream of tartar and salt until thick and foamy.

Increase speed to high, add vinegar and gradually add the sugar in 5 separate batches, beating well between each. Continue beating until stiff peaks have formed and sugar has dissolved. Fold in cornflour and vanilla.

Using a large kitchen spoon, place large spoonfuls of mixture onto the tray around 5cm/2 inches apart.

Place into an oven and bake for 1 hour. Reduce temperature to 70°C/160°F and cook for a further 30 minutes to 1 hour or until dry to touch. Turn oven off, leaving pavlovas in the oven for at least another hour, or overnight. To store, place into an airtight container, they will keep for 2-3 days.

To serve, place on a plate and top with fresh whipped cream, pour over passionfruit pulp and scatter with fresh berries and mint.

Strawberries, kiwi fruit and shaved chocolate are always a great combination too.

Peach Bellini (Cocktail)

Serves: 8

This is my take on the world famous Harry's bar Peach Bellini.

This recipe allows for a little preparation done in advance without the peach turning brown. Classically made with white peaches (my favourite), however I have in the past used yellow, still very refreshing.

This is a seasonal drink due to stone fruit being at there best during the summer months. There are however tetra packs of fruit purees on the market now that make a drink like this available all year round. Tinned peaches can also be used.

6 white peaches (or 12 halves of tinned peaches)
500gm sugar
2L water
1 bottle champagne

Bring a large pot of water to the boil, Plunge peaches into the boiling water for 20 seconds then remove to a bowl iced water. Peel away the skin from the peaches.

In a pot mix together sugar and water, add in peaches cover with parchment paper, place over heat and bring to the boil and simmer for 2 minutes. Remove from heat allowing to cool.

Before serving, slice cooked peaches in half, remove stone and puree in a blender adding a little of the poaching liquor to thin out.

To serve fill a champagne flute ⅓ full then top with ice cold champagne.

elementsindex

G'day,

I hope you're enjoying *Elements* and have learnt a few new tricks from the DVD! I really did have a lot of fun putting this project together, with the help of my team at *Manic J Productions*. *Manic J* is a new operation that my business partner, Maree Gadd, and I set up in 2005. Under the *Manic J* banner we've published this book and plan to do several more in the future. We're also creating a cool range of homewares and gourmet foods, plus we're constantly developing and writing new television shows.

To find out more about all this, why not check out what's happening in our manic world at **www.manicj.com**. You'll find heaps of info on our products, including barbecue planks, TV cooking shows, cooking schools and classes as well as when and where I'll be appearing. Hopefully somewhere near your place real soon. And when you're on the site, make sure you sign-up for our newsletter and special offers too.

See ya,

Jase

MANICJ
PRODUCTIONS

www.manicj.com

productionelements

I'd just like to say a very big thank you to everyone associated with the production of this book and DVD. Guys, you're all awesome.

Jase

Sunjay Jain (Sun of Jay)... a million thanks for your long-standing support. You believe in me always and inspire Maree and I to do more, to do better and to never give up. For all the long hours, location managing, early mornings, late nights, weekend gigs, computer problems, bogged vans, website and domain issues, support of Maree, pick ups and deliveries, summer swims, beers and great lunches, thank you!

Nicola Francis, thank you for all your support. You are always there with a smile and your work in the past for Manic J is appreciated.

Peter Everett, thank you for your continued and long-standing friendship. You are always there with good advice, open arms and open ears. Your spirituality gives me peace. Thank you also for arranging the Kangaroo Valley location at such short notice, it's greatly appreciated.

Locations, Locations, Locations.

Thanks to **Gavin Greenstone of Filmsite** for assisting in our arduous searches for "Elements" locations.

Fuzzy for the fabulous Cottage Point location that made us feel a million miles from civilization. We have shot your house a few times, but never yet have we had time to relax and enjoy it! Your vision and labour of love building the house was well worth it and we thank you.

Charles for allowing us into your amazing and stylish Sydney Penthouse for our dinner party shoot. All the crew are still adamant they want to live there. Thank you also for all your kindness and generosity during the shoot, it was greatly appreciated.

Tony White and Alex Michael for allowing us into your breathtaking and serene Kangaroo Valley oasis for our BBQ shoot. Despite getting bogged and torrential rain, the skies opened up and gave us beautiful views and sunshine, showing us the beauty you see every day. Particular thanks for allowing us to shoot at such short notice... and special thanks to Alex for his continuing work on Manic J projects... only you would know a colander could be a light fitting!

Produce and ingredients

This book could not have been possible without the fantastic produce, ingredients and homewares from **Matt Brown's Greens, Vic's Meats, Sydney Fish Market, De Costi Seafood, Breville and Alex Liddy.**

The team at **Matt Brown's Greens...** for choosing picture perfect produce each and every day of the shoot. To Matt, a personal thanks for years of working together in the Sydney restaurant scene.

Anthony Puharich and the team at **Vic's Meats...** come flood, rain or snow, you will always make sure I get my meat. For allowing us to shoot the DVD at your place, I hope this will open the world's eyes to the fantastic quality of Vic's Premium Quality Meats... and yes Anthony, I know I still owe you dinner... and it will be real soon.

Amber Forrest-Bisley and Graham Turk from Sydney Fish Market for your organisation and participation in the seafood section of the DVD. I am looking forward to the world seeing what a fabulous fish market Sydney has... here's to many more great meals cooked with Australian seafood.

Tony Muollo at De Costi Seafood (Trans Tasman Fisheries) for your belief in this book, your fabulous on-camera work showing the world your produce and for always being so accommodating whilst we were disrupting your store with camera crews.

thankyou

I owe a million thanks to many people for making this book a reality. Me without my team is like a man without a country. This is my first self publishing endeavour so it has taken many, many hours and late nights to get this book to the shelves, but I have an amazing feeling of self-satisfaction and accomplishment. Although I am the author of Elements, it is the visions of the team around me that have given life to this project also. To them I will remain eternally grateful and cherish the long hours and days we spent together.

Some people in particular I would like to thank…

Thank you to **my family** for all the unconditional love, trust and support you give me each and every day, you drive me to want to succeed. Thank you.

Kisses and squeezes to my much loved son **Hunter** who has to put up with his Dad's schedule of traveling the world juggling several projects at once. I hope this book inspires you to cook and grow with an open mind. Words cannot begin to explain the love I have for you. The time we share together is unforgettable and very precious to me.

Maree Gadd...without you this book would not breathe, my recipes would be without a home. How do I thank you Maree Gadd, my friend, business partner and 24-hour emergency support line. Without your tireless commitment to our company Manic J and your constant ability to conquer any obstacle, this book would not have been created and Manic J would not be delving into so many exciting new areas. Your consistent knowledge and ideas amaze me, always thinking of new concepts and solutions 24/7… Do you ever sleep?

You have made this ambitious self-publishing dream a reality for both of us. Thank you for your tireless support, ambition and ability to make things happen. Thank you for the half time rolls filled with mortadella, salami and prosciutto, a million gallons of mango and pineapple juice, not to mention the 3 o'clock snack. You are a force to be reckoned with, which allows me the time and space to be creative in the kitchen.

Here's to many years of memorable Manic J missions.

Tom Howing… A world of thanks for allowing me to… throw endless amounts of snow at Nick, Andrew and Matthew, dance with your wife Mary (Hi Mary) and reside at Hotel Howing. You took me to my very first ice hockey game, you support me and believe in me constantly. For this I will always be thankful… and the 2 tickets to the Emmy's® may come sooner than you think!

Damian Pignolet… To my friend and mentor, thank you for opening the many doors you have in my lifetime. Your patience, understanding and love for food and friends inspires me every day. I feel privileged and blessed to be able to call you my friend.

The Alticor and iCook teams who have had a large part in making this book a reality… Andy Gamm, Dale Selvius, David Madiol, Sue Reahm, Sue Hoff and of course, Steve Palazzolo, the legal eagle. Special thanks to the DeVos and Van Andel families for their constant support.

Garnet Meekings and Cathriona Kelly at Fox Badger Ferret… your vision for the book was perfection. Your work for Manic J and myself is always amazing, we don't know how you do it, but you do. It is always such a great pleasure working with you and thank you for the long and tireless hours you spent with us in the studio and back at "ground zero" 'til all hours of the night and morning putting this book together on an extremely tight deadline. I look forward to many more books and projects with you!

oliverford
photography
oliverford.com.au

Oliver Ford... two words, brilliant photographer. Thanks for shooting with a square eye! For all the days and nights we spent together over the 11+ day shoot, it was lots of fun and I really enjoyed working with you. The only photographer I know who can shoot 22+ recipes a day and still look cool… I think it was the endless supply of Caramello Santa's that did it! Here's to the next book and the world (and you) knowing what a great photographer you are!

Mark Kuzma... my stylish stylist… for your visions, your style, your taste, your connections, your laugh, your never ending energy, your abilities as a chef and your friendship, a million thanks. When I would pick you up in the morning it never felt like we were going to shoot a book, it felt like we were on the way to a building site, who knew how many sheets of roofing, glass, wood, tiles, planks and stools, pictures, crates, barrels vases etc would fit in my car!

I couldn't have done it without you.

HALT
HAIR & BEAUTY

Daniel McLennan and the team at Halt Hair and Beauty... For many years you have always made sure my hair was right, my nails were well kept and I always looked the part. For this, countless other things and for your long standing friendship, I thank you. A day with you on the set is one the whole crew looks forward too, filled with lots of laughs and Sudoku and your endless quest to learn the ins and outs of every location we shoot… here's to many more great years.

Vanessa Horton... thanks for the prep, cutting, chopping, dicing, peeling, cooking, fun, laughs, help and the millions of dishes you washed… you were a fantastic help and I look forward to working with you again.

Christine Sheppard... the queen of the red pen and online editing, thanks for all the millions of conversions you did, the rocket to arugala and trying to explain my methods of madness (and ingredients) so the rest of the world would understand them.

Blacksheep
PRODUCTIONS

Ben Alcott and the team at Blacksheep Productions... a big thank you for all your work, for putting up with lighting issues as always, sand, sun, rain, surf and all the early mornings, we look forward to a long future working together.

David Salzburg and the team at Mandalay Integrated Media Entertainment, your support of myself and Manic J Productions' work means a great deal to me and my team and I feel very blessed to be working with you, a million thanks.

The Team at BDO, Sydney – Geoff Taylor, Leo Cohilj and the wonderful Fiona Lyon for all your continued support and making sure the money side of things – here and overseas, always works out! You are very valuable members of the Manic J team.

Rupert Rosenblum... for many years of support and handling the legalities of our Australian operations so professionally, for being the final proof-reader of this book… and of course for your continuing love of good food, thank you.

Michael Conley... thank you for your professionalism, legal knowledge and advice, it will always be remembered.

The U.S. Officials... Shawn Eyestone of Law Weathers and Richardson, Kathy Hanenburg and the team of Warner Norcross & Judd and Larry Conroy of Deloitte USA for all your continual work – we couldn't do it without you!

Sunjay Jain (Sun of Jay)... a million thanks for your long-standing support. You believe in me always and inspire Maree and I to do more, to do better and to never give up. For all the long hours, location managing, early mornings, late nights, weekend gigs, computer problems, bogged vans, website and domain issues, support of Maree, pick ups and deliveries, summer swims, beers and great lunches, thank you!

Nicola Francis, thank you for all your support. You are always there with a smile and your work in the past for Manic J is appreciated.

Peter Everett, thank you for your continued and long-standing friendship. You are always there with good advice, open arms and open ears. Your spirituality gives me peace. Thank you also for arranging the Kangaroo Valley location at such short notice, it's greatly appreciated.

Locations, Locations, Locations.

Thanks to ***Gavin Greenstone of Filmsite*** for assisting in our arduous searches for "Elements" locations.

Fuzzy for the fabulous Cottage Point location that made us feel a million miles from civilization. We have shot your house a few times, but never yet have we had time to relax and enjoy it! Your vision and labour of love building the house was well worth it and we thank you.

Charles for allowing us into your amazing and stylish Sydney Penthouse for our dinner party shoot. All the crew are still adamant they want to live there. Thank you also for all your kindness and generosity during the shoot, it was greatly appreciated.

Tony White and Alex Michael for allowing us into your breathtaking and serene Kangaroo Valley oasis for our BBQ shoot. Despite getting bogged and torrential rain, the skies opened up and gave us beautiful views and sunshine, showing us the beauty you see every day. Particular thanks for allowing us to shoot at such short notice... and special thanks to Alex for his continuing work on Manic J projects... only you would know a colander could be a light fitting!

Produce and ingredients

This book could not have been possible without the fantastic produce, ingredients and homewares from ***Matt Brown's Greens, Vic's Meats, Sydney Fish Market, De Costi Seafood, Breville and Alex Liddy.***

The team at ***Matt Brown's Greens...*** for choosing picture perfect produce each and every day of the shoot. To Matt, a personal thanks for years of working together in the Sydney restaurant scene.

Anthony Puharich and the team at ***Vic's Meats...*** come flood, rain or snow, you will always make sure I get my meat. For allowing us to shoot the DVD at your place, I hope this will open the world's eyes to the fantastic quality of Vic's Premium Quality Meats... and yes Anthony, I know I still owe you dinner... and it will be real soon.

Amber Forrest-Bisley and Graham Turk from Sydney Fish Market for your organisation and participation in the seafood section of the DVD. I am looking forward to the world seeing what a fabulous fish market Sydney has... here's to many more great meals cooked with Australian seafood.

Tony Muollo at De Costi Seafood (Trans Tasman Fisheries) for your belief in this book, your fabulous on-camera work showing the world your produce and for always being so accommodating whilst we were disrupting your store with camera crews.

John Cunnington from The Art of Food and Wine for the fabulous kitchenware and homewares, I could spend days in your store and give my credit card a good workout… I feel I need one of everything!

Golden Century Restaurant my home away from home

Les Gyorfi – my fantastic cooking teacher at East Sydney Technical Institute,

Simon Johnson, Chef's Warehouse, Maggi Beer and her wonderful Verjuice, **Pino**, **Pia** and the entire **Tomini-Foresti family from Dolce Vita Fine Foods** in Kogarah – your meat is amazing and your friendship appreciated. I'm looking forward to many Italian food tours with you!

Gayle at Coles Sylvania

The friendly parking rangers and parking inspectors of Sydney who found it in their good hearts to give me a plethora of parking tickets throughout the shooting of this book.

Sadie Daoud and Nahrain Isaac from Westpac Private Bank… our lifesavers. You have both had such an impact on this book and your work is greatly appreciated. Thank you for your belief in us and this project… we look forward to many more years of Manic J projects with you.

Anna Lindsay, Michael Good, Jason Stevens, Angela Stevens, Peter Everett, Tony White, Alex Michael and Peter Litynski for being my stylish guests in the DVD.

To **Justin Zammit** – from one chef to another… thank you for all your help… here's to lots more adventures (not involving bogged minibuses though)… and here's wishing you and Amy many happy years together.

To those people who parted with their special recipes: **Shen Tan** for her Singapore Chilli Mud Crab and **Pat Feige** for his pasta sauce, I thank you.

To every chef I have had the privilege of working next to in the kitchen and for those who have welcomed me into their kitchen on my international work, I thank you.

Jase

Published by Love Me Tender Pty Ltd Trading as Manic J Productions

Manic J Productions

PO Box 732
Rozelle NSW 2039
Australia
Email: elements@manicj.com

Love Me Tender LLC

LWR PC
800 Bridgewater Place
333 Bridge Street NW
Grand Rapids MI 49504-5320
Incorp

Elements Book

Publisher	Jason Roberts
Editor	Maree Gadd
Photography	Oliver Ford
Food Styling	Marc Kuzma
Design Consultants	Fox Badger Ferret Pty Limited
Creative Director	Garnet Meekings
Designer/Art Director	Cathriona Kelly
Graphic Artist	Paul Mackey
Food Editor	Christine Sheppard
Food Preparation	Vanessa Horton
Hair & Make Up Artist	Daniel McLennan, Halt Hair & Beauty

Elements DVD

Production Company	Blacksheep Productions
Director	Ben Alcott
Camera	Ben Alcott
	Tony Marinceski
	Paul Hamcides
Sound	George Davis
Post Production	Gavin Walters
	Elizabeth Briedis
Executive Producer	Jason Roberts
Producer	Maree Gadd
Production Assistant	Nicola Francis
Photography	Oliver Ford
Hair & Make Up Artist	Daniel McLennan, Halt Hair & Beauty

The publisher would like to thank Breville, Alex Liddy, HWI Electrical, iCook, De Costi Seafood, Vic's Meats and Smeg for supplying props, kitchenware and produce for this book.

National Library of Australia Cataloguing-in-Publication Data
Roberts, Jason, 1971–. Elements: Food. Includes Index.
ISBN 0 9775111 0 3 1. Cookery I. Title 641.5

Printed by BrightFerry Printing & Packing Ltd. Printed in Shenzhen, China. First published 2006.
Text copyright © Manic J Productions.
Design and photography copyright © Manic J Productions 2005.

All rights reserved. No part of this publication may be reproduced, stored in a retrieval system or transmitted in any form or by any means, electronic, mechanical, photocopying, recording or otherwise without the prior written permission of the publisher.

Please note some ingredients may contain traces of nuts.

Conversion guide: Cooking times vary depending on the oven being used. For fan-forced ovens, as a general rule, set the oven temperature to 20°C (35°F) lower than indicated in the recipe.

We have used 20ml (4 teaspoon) tablespoon measures. If you are using a 15ml (3 teaspoon) tablespoon, for most recipes the difference will not be noticeable. However for recipes using baking powder, gelatine, bicarbonate of soda (baking soda) or a small amount of cornflour (cornstarch), add an extra teaspoon for each tablespoon specified. We have also used 60g (2oz) eggs.